Social Anxiety Disorder

About the Authors

Martin M. Antony, PhD, is Professor in the Department of Psychology at Ryerson University in Toronto. He is also Director of Research at the Anxiety Treatment and Research Centre at St. Joseph's Healthcare in Hamilton, Ontario. Dr. Antony has published more than 20 books and 100 scientific articles and book chapters in the areas of anxiety disorders and cognitive behavior therapy. His contributions to research and training have been recognized by awards from the Society of Clinical Psychology, the Canadian Psychological Association, and a number of other professional organizations.

Karen Rowa, PhD, is a psychologist at the Anxiety Treatment and Research Centre at St. Joseph's Healthcare in Hamilton, Ontario and an Assistant Professor in the Department of Psychiatry and Behavioral Neurosciences at McMaster University in Hamilton. She is active in teaching and supervising students in the assessment and cognitive behavioral treatment of anxiety and related disorders. She has published a number of scientific articles and book chapters in the area of anxiety disorders and cognitive behavior therapy, and is the coauthor of two books.

Advances in Psychotherapy – Evidence-Based Practice

Danny Wedding; PhD, MPH, Prof., St. Louis, MO
(Series Editor)
Larry Beutler; PhD, Prof., Palo Alto, CA
Kenneth E. Freedland; PhD, Prof., St. Louis, MO
Linda C. Sobell; PhD, ABPP, Prof., Ft. Lauderdale, FL
David A. Wolfe; PhD, Prof., Toronto
(Associate Editors)

The basic objective of this series is to provide therapists with practical, evidence-based treatment guidance for the most common disorders seen in clinical practice – and to do so in a "reader-friendly" manner. Each book in the series is both a compact "how-to-do" reference on a particular disorder for use by professional clinicians in their daily work, as well as an ideal educational resource for students and for practice-oriented continuing education.

The most important feature of the books is that they are practical and "reader-friendly:" All are structured similarly and all provide a compact and easy-to-follow guide to all aspects that are relevant in real-life practice. Tables, boxed clinical "pearls", marginal notes, and summary boxes assist orientation, while checklists provide tools for use in daily practice.

Social Anxiety Disorder

Martin M. Antony
Department of Psychology, Ryerson University, Toronto, ON

Karen Rowa
Department of Psychiatry and Behavioral Neurosciences, McMaster University, Hamilton, ON

Library of Congress Cataloging in Publication

is available via the Library of Congress Marc Database under the
LC Control Number 2007938580

Library and Archives Canada Cataloguing in Publication

Antony, Martin M. (Martin Mitchell)
    Social anxiety disorder / Martin M. Antony, Karen Rowa.

(Advances in psychotherapy–evidence-based practice)
Includes bibliographical references.
ISBN 978-0-88937-311-2

    1. Social phobia. 2. Social phobia–Treatment. I. Rowa, Karen, 1974-
II. Title. III. Series.

RC552.S62A68 2008   616.85'225   C2007-906456-6

PUBLISHING OFFICES
USA: Hogrefe & Huber Publishers, 875 Massachusetts Avenue, 7th Floor,
                 Cambridge, MA 02139
                 Phone (866) 823-4726, Fax (617) 354-6875; E-mail info@hhpub.com
EUROPE: Hogrefe & Huber Publishers, Rohnsweg 25, 37085 Göttingen, Germany
                 Phone +49 551 49609-0, Fax +49 551 49609-88, E-mail hh@hhpub.com

SALES & DISTRIBUTION
USA: Hogrefe & Huber Publishers, Customer Services Department,
                 30 Amberwood Parkway, Ashland, OH 44805
                 Phone (800) 228-3749, Fax (419) 281-6883, E-mail custserv@hhpub.com
EUROPE: Hogrefe & Huber Publishers, Rohnsweg 25, 37085 Göttingen, Germany
                 Phone +49 551 49609-0, Fax +49 551 49609-88, E-mail hh@hhpub.com

OTHER OFFICES
CANADA: Hogrefe & Huber Publishers, 1543 Bayview Avenue, Toronto, Ontario M4G
3B5
SWITZERLAND: Hogrefe & Huber Publishers, Länggass-Strasse 76, CH-3000 Bern 9

Hogrefe & Huber Publishers
Incorporated and registered in the State of Washington, USA, and in Göttingen, Lower Saxony,
Germany

Printed and bound in the USA
ISBN 978-0-88937-311-2

Preface

Social anxiety disorder (SAD; also called *social phobia*) is one of the most common psychological disorders which, left untreated, can lead to significant impairment in a person's life and significant societal costs. Fortunately, there are effective treatments for SAD, including pharmacological and psychological interventions. This book describes the components of an empirically supported psychological therapy for SAD, namely cognitive behavioral therapy (CBT). CBT includes exposure techniques, cognitive techniques, and social skills training, and all of these treatment components are described in detail in this book. This book is intended for a variety of mental health professionals who see individuals with SAD in their practices, including psychologists, psychiatrists, social workers, family physicians, other mental health professionals, and trainees in all of these disciplines.

This book is divided into six chapters. The first two chapters are designed to provide a theoretical and descriptive overview of SAD. Chapter 1 reviews topics such as prevalence, comorbidity, and differential diagnosis. SAD has features that overlap with other psychological disorders, and a clear diagnostic picture is necessary for treatment purposes. We outline some of the most common differential diagnoses one should consider when assessing and diagnosing SAD. In Chapter 2, we review the leading theoretical models and research on the development and maintenance of SAD, including both cognitive behavioral models as well as genetic and developmental theories. Chapter 3 provides an overview of the key domains of assessment one should consider when seeing someone with SAD. It is not enough to simply establish a diagnosis of SAD; to effectively plan treatment interventions one needs to assess a number of important domains of symptoms, avoidance, etc. In Chapter 4, CBT techniques for SAD are described. Practical strategies are outlined for clinicians, and the empirical support for these strategies is reviewed. Although clinical illustrations are interspersed throughout this book, Chapter 5 is dedicated to two clinical vignettes where treatment is described from start to finish. Finally, Chapter 6 includes suggestions for further reading for the interested individual and useful forms are included in the Appendix.

Empirical support for cognitive behavioral treatment for SAD is encouraging. However, not all clinicians have access to training and supervision in this type of treatment. We hope that books such as this can help to bridge the divide between empirically supported treatments and day-to-day practice. Ideally, a book such as this would be used as one of several tools in learning the application of cognitive behavioral techniques to anxiety-related problems such as social anxiety, in conjunction with other readings, continuing education workshops and courses, case discussion and consultation with colleagues, and opportunities for supervision.

Our understanding of the nature and treatment of SAD has been influenced by the work of numerous experts, including Aaron T. Beck, Deborah Beidel, David M. Clark, Edna Foa, Richard Heimberg, Ron Rapee, Samuel Turner,

Adrian Wells, and many others. Our clinical examples and experiences have been mainly gathered through working with clients at the Anxiety Treatment and Research Centre (ATRC) at St. Joseph's Healthcare in Hamilton, Ontario. It has been immensely rewarding to watch so many individuals reclaim their lives and learn to manage their symptoms of anxiety though the implementation of CBT techniques. We are also grateful to the staff at the ATRC for supporting and participating in all the clinical and research endeavors that have helped us advance our clinical and theoretical knowledge of SAD.

We would like to thank Dr. Danny Wedding, as well as Robert Dimbleby of Hogrefe and Huber Publishers for inviting us to participate in what we believe is a timely and important series on empirically supported therapies for a range of psychological, psychiatric, and physical conditions. We appreciate their flexibility, patience, and guidance in the writing of this book. Finally, we would like to thank our families for their continued encouragement and support.

Martin M. Antony, PhD
Toronto, ON, Canada

Karen Rowa, PhD
Hamilton, ON, Canada

Dedication

For my granddaughter, Parker
MMA

For my parents, Ellen and Doug Rowa
KR

Table of Contents

1

Description

1.1   Terminology

Social anxiety disorder (SAD; also called *social phobia)* is characterized by an intense fear of social or performance situations. In these situations, people with SAD are worried about embarrassment, humiliation, or scrutiny by others. Although many people are nervous or shy in social or performance situations (e.g., some studies suggest that 40% of individuals consider themselves to be chronically shy; Henderson & Zimbardo, 1998), SAD is diagnosed when this anxiety becomes so intense and pervasive that it causes significant distress for a person or it impairs the person's ability to function (e.g., at work or school, in relationships, etc.). Some situations that people with SAD often fear include:

- Conversations
- Meeting new people
- Calling acquaintances or strangers on the telephone
- Parties
- Talking to authority figures
- Expressing a controversial opinion or disagreement
- Being assertive
- Speaking in front of a group
- Participating in meetings
- Entering a crowded room
- Being the center of attention
- Eating or drinking in front of others
- Writing in front of others
- Making mistakes in front of others

The number of situations feared by people with SAD varies from person to person. Some people report concerns about a few situations, or even just one particular situation (e.g., public speaking) whereas others indicate fear across a broad range of social and performance situations.

People with SAD fear and avoid situations due to anxiety over the possibility of being embarrassed or judged by others

1.2   Definition

The major classification scheme that provides a definition of and criteria for diagnosing SAD is the text revision of the fourth edition of the *Diagnostic and Statistical Manual of Mental Disorders* (DSM-IV-TR; American Psychiatric Association, 2000). The DSM-IV-TR views SAD categorically, meaning that criteria for the disorder are either met or not met. Of course, even though the diagnostic criteria are categorical, social anxiety exists on a continuum from mild shyness to severe symptoms. In severe cases of social anxiety, criteria for avoidant personality disorder (APD) may also be met. In fact, some authors have argued that there is such substantial overlap between severe SAD and APD that it may not be useful to consider them as distinct conditions. Indeed, there are few cases in which an individual is diagnosed with APD *without* a corresponding diagnosis of SAD. Studies suggest no differences between the disorders with respect to parental history of social anxiety, with both disorders showing a two to three-fold increase in risk of social anxiety if family history was positive for social anxiety (Tillfors, Furmark, Ekselius, & Fredrikson, 2001). However, a number of studies have found that there are other significant differences between individuals with just SAD versus those with both SAD and APD, suggesting that there is more that separates these groups than simply their level of social anxiety (Hofmann & Barlow, 2002). Further, authors have argued that these syndromes should remain distinct because SAD is a treatable disorder while outcomes for APD are less optimistic (Wittchen & Fehm, 2003). Statistical procedures, such as structural equation modeling, also support the conceptual distinction of these constructs (Strunk, Huppert, Foa, & Davidson, 2003). Clinically, it can be difficult to disentangle these syndromes, leaving a clinician unsure whether a client has both disorders, versus simply one or the other. Later in this chapter, we outline strategies that clinicians can use to differentiate between SAD and APD.

In DSM-IV-TR, SAD is defined as a marked and persistent fear of one or more social situations that often leads to avoidance of the feared situations. The individual fears being humiliated, scrutinized, or embarrassed. This fear must occur upon most exposures to social situations (i.e., it cannot be a transient fear), and the person must recognize that the fear is excessive. Some individuals may experience cued panic attacks in social situations (e.g., either when they are in the situation or when they are anticipating an upcoming stressful situation). Symptoms of social anxiety must lead to significant distress for the individual, or impairment in the person's life. Examples of ways that SAD may cause functional impairment for sufferers include social or marital problems (e.g., few friends, marital tension due to one's inability to attend social events, inability to date), employment or academic activities (e.g., inability to get a job due to fears of interviews, lack of advancement in one's current job due to anxiety, missed days of work, or missed classes), and day-to-day functioning (e.g., inability to make important phone calls, avoidance of public places). Impairment in SAD can be severe. Indeed, individuals with SAD report greater functional impairment than individuals with a variety of medical conditions including end-state renal failure (Antony, Roth, Swinson, Huta, & Devins, 1998) and genital herpes (Wittchen & Beloch, 1996). Functional impairment can lead to serious consequences. For example, one of our clients with SAD was not collecting disability payments he was entitled to because of fears of being criticized by others if he applied, as well as strong anxiety about making phone calls to "strangers" to request an application. Due to this inability to override his anxiety and apply for support, he found himself falling into significant debt.

According to DSM-IV-TR, the term "generalized" should be used to describe cases of SAD in which an individual reports fear in *most* social or

> **In severe cases, people with SAD may be unable to work and may have no close friends**

performance situations. Although no specific rules are provided for how many situations constitute "most" social situations, this subtype appears to be a reliable and valid way of distinguishing between individuals with more pervasive SAD versus those whose fear is limited to a small number of situations (e.g., public speaking).

1.3   Epidemiology

SAD appears to be one of the most common psychological disorders, though prevalence rates in the literature vary across studies. For example, lifetime prevalence estimates for SAD based on large community samples in the United States range from 3 to 13% (Antony & Swinson, 2000; Kessler et al., 2005; Somers, Goldner, Waraich, & Hsu, 2006). One factor that may account for the variability across studies is the diagnostic instrument used to assess SAD. For example, older studies based on DSM-III criteria (e.g., Eaton, Dryman, & Weissman, 1991), tended to assess fear in a relatively small number of social situations, compared to newer studies based on DSM-III-R (Kessler et al., 1994) or DSM-IV (Kessler et al., 2005) criteria. When a greater number of social situations are provided as prompts for individuals, prevalence rates tend to be higher. Prevalence rates also vary depending on ways in which distress and impairment are measured in SAD, the age composition of the sample, and the cultural composition of the sample (Wittchen & Fehm, 2003).

SAD tends to begin in adolescence (i.e., mid to late teens), but can also occur earlier in childhood. In fact, significant numbers of adults report that they have had problems with social anxiety for their entire lives or as long as they can remember. A large-scale study of individuals presenting at an anxiety clinic found a mean age of onset of 15.7 years, a number that was younger than the age of onset of the other anxiety disorders (Brown, Campbell, Lehman, Grisham, & Mancill, 2001). Studies suggest that SAD is associated with similar or related problems in childhood, including selective mutism, school refusal, separation anxiety, and shyness (Albano & Detweiler, 2001). Since most studies employ retrospective data from adults, it is unclear whether SAD, per se, would have been diagnosed in childhood for these individuals or whether individuals believe that they had SAD in childhood because they were dealing with a host of related problems that later developed into SAD. Nevertheless, SAD is routinely diagnosed in specialty anxiety clinics for children, validating the fact that this disorder commonly begins in childhood or adolescence. Cases of SAD beginning in later adulthood are rare and may actually be social anxiety secondary to another mental disorder (e.g., social withdrawal in depression, avoidance of eating in public in an eating disorder).

Epidemiological studies suggest that SAD is slightly more common in women than in men (Fehm, Pelissolo, Furmark, & Wittchen, 2005), though these differences appear especially small when compared to gender differences for other anxiety disorders where women are commonly overrepresented (e.g., panic disorder, specific phobias, generalized anxiety disorder). Gender differences in clinical samples are negligible, and some evidence even suggests that men may be more likely to present for treatment (Hofmann & Barlow, 2002).

SAD is slightly more prevalent in women than men

There are some gender differences in the presentation of SAD. For example, men and women differ in their most feared social situations. Turk et al. (1998) found that women were more fearful than men of talking to people in authority, performing in front of an audience, working while being observed, entering a room where others are already seated, being the center of attention, speaking at meetings, expressing disagreement, giving a report to a group, and throwing ·a party. In contrast, men were more fearful than women of returning goods to a store and urinating in a public bathroom.

SAD is a broad cultural phenomenon, appearing in such diverse cultures as Japan, Korea, Australia, Sweden, Saudi Arabia, and other East Asian countries. Although the general presentation of SAD is fairly consistent across cultures, there are some interesting cultural differences. For example, the types of situations that produce anxiety differ across cultures. One study compared people with SAD from Sweden, Australia, and the United States (Heimberg, Makris, Juster, Öst, & Rapee, 1997). Results suggested that Swedish individuals were more fearful of situations involving public observation (e.g., writing in public, eating or drinking in public, and public speaking). Individuals from Australia were more fearful of dating and starting conversations. Another study comparing individuals with SAD from the United States, Canada, Puerto Rico, and Korea found that fears of speaking to strangers were more pronounced in the Korean sample than in the other groups (Weissman et al., 1996). Another cultural difference is that SAD appears to be less prevalent in the Far East than in Western countries (e.g., Hwu, Yeh, & Chang, 1989). It is possible that socially reserved and introverted behaviors are more socially acceptable in Eastern countries that focus on "collectivism" rather than individualistic pursuits. It is also possible that Eastern cultures have more reserved attitudes about revealing personal information in interview situations.

In Japan and Korea, individuals may suffer from *taijin kyofusho syndrome* (TKS), which is similar to SAD except that individuals with TKS are concerned about doing something that may offend or embarrass *others* rather than themselves. For example, an individual with TKS may worry that he will offend others by emitting an unpleasant odor, by staring at others, or by making an improper facial expression. It has been suggested that TKS is an East Asian form of SAD that emerges from the societal emphasis on collectivism (Kirmayer, 1991). In other words, culture is seen to affect the form in which social anxiety symptoms present. Thus, it is not enough to simply identify a person's feared situations when assessing SAD, but it is also imperative to understand the *focus* of a person's fear, particularly when working with clients of Asian descent.

Most studies of SAD have been based in Western countries, though there are a few studies that have examined cross-cultural differences

1.4   Course and Prognosis

Left untreated, SAD appears to have a chronic, unremitting course and it often precedes the development of other psychological disorders, such as depression and substance use (Stein et al., 2001). One study followed individuals with SAD for 65 weeks and found that very few individuals achieved remission from their disorder during this time frame. The subtypes of generalized versus nongeneralized did not differ in this regard (Reich, Goldenberg, Vasile, Goisman, & Keller, 1994). Furthermore, the severity of SAD did not affect its course. In other words, individuals with severe SAD experienced the same low level of remission as those with mild SAD. Other studies echo these findings, suggesting that the chance of achieving remission in SAD is less than the likelihood of recovery for other anxiety disorders (Yonkers, Bruce, Dyck, & Keller, 2003). Additionally, the presence of a comorbid personality disorder (e.g., avoidant personality disorder) leads to even lower rates of remission for individuals with SAD (Massion et al., 2002). Unfortunately, there are consequences of the unremitting course of SAD, including greater lifetime disability and a higher risk of suicide attempts for individuals with SAD (20% risk of suicide attempts) compared to those without SAD (8%; Keller, 2003).

Fortunately, there are a number of successful interventions that can affect the course and outcome of SAD. Cognitive behavioral therapy (CBT) has been identified as an empirically-supported psychological treatment for SAD. Studies suggest that individuals who receive CBT experience significant improvements in both symptoms as well as the level of functional impairment caused by SAD. Chapter 4 includes more detailed information on the efficacy of CBT for SAD. Further, there are a number of pharmacological agents that have demonstrated success in treating SAD. Therapeutic intervention can dramatically alter an otherwise pessimistic course for SAD.

1.5   Differential Diagnosis

There are a number of disorders with overlapping or similar features to SAD, making diagnosing this disorder difficult at times. The following section aims to highlight both the similarities and differences between SAD and the following disorders: panic disorder with agoraphobia (PDA), generalized anxiety disorder (GAD), particular specific phobias (i.e., crowds, enclosed places), depression, avoidant personality disorder, and schizoid personality disorder.

> **Anxiety in social situations is a feature of many different psychological disorders in addition to SAD** .

1.5.1   Panic Disorder with Agoraphobia

There are a number of similarities between PDA and SAD. Both disorders are characterized by avoidance, and the situations avoided are often similar across these disorders; For example, both disorders may be associated with avoidance of situations like crowds, parties, or public places. To distinguish between these disorders, it is important to examine the underlying reasons for avoidance. In prototypic cases, people with PDA avoid situations for fear of having a panic attack or panic like symptoms, whereas people with SAD often avoid situations for fear of being humiliated or criticized for reasons unrelated to panic (e.g., being seen as incompetent, boring, unattractive, overly nervous, weak, stupid, etc.). Differential diagnosis is complicated, however, because some people with PD are concerned about embarrassing themselves if they have a panic attack in front of others, and some people with SAD are fearful of experiencing panic attacks or panic-like symptoms. To disentangle panic-related concerns from SAD, it is helpful to consider the following information: (a) Does the person experience panic attacks and panic-like symptoms outside of social situations (e.g., when alone), or out of the blue? Uncued panic attacks and panic attacks cued by nonsocial situations are common in PDA, but in SAD panic attacks and panic-like symptoms are triggered only by being in or thinking about being in social situations. (b) Does the individual have panic related concerns that are unrelated to being embarrassed or humiliated (e.g., a fear of dying or going crazy)? This is often the case in PDA, but not in SAD. (c) Does the person have social anxiety concerns that are unrelated to a fear of having panic attacks (e.g., fear of saying something stupid or looking unattractive to others)? This is often the case in SAD, but not in PDA. Of course, individuals who have uncued panic attacks outside of social situations, as well as extreme fears of criticism and embarrassment that are unrelated to panic may receive diagnoses of both PDA and SAD.

> **Panic attacks cued by social situations are common among individuals with SAD**

Another similarity between PDA and SAD involves elevated anxiety sensitivity, which refers to anxiety over experiencing sensations of physical arousal, such as a racing heart, dizziness, and breathlessness. Although anxiety sensitivity is seen as a hallmark feature of PDA, studies suggest that these concerns are often elevated in SAD, though typically not as high as in PDA (Taylor, Koch, & McNally, 1992). A commonly used questionnaire for anxiety sensitivity is the Anxiety Sensitivity Index (Peterson and Reiss, 1993), and there are several variations of this scale available as well (e.g., Taylor & Cox, 1998; Taylor et al., 2007). In our experience, people with SAD are most likely to fear sensations that might be noticed by others (e.g., blushing, sweating, shaking), and they are most fearful of experiencing physical arousal sensations when they are around other people. In contrast, people with PDA are more likely to fear a range of sensations, even when alone (and for some people, *especially* when alone).

1.5.2   Generalized Anxiety Disorder

SAD and GAD may both share heightened or excessive worry about social situations, performance situations, and relationships. For example, people with GAD often worry about friendships, whether their relationships will work out, and how they appear to others. Further, people with both SAD and GAD may avoid these situations due to elevated levels of anxiety. As in SAD, people with GAD may experience panic attacks when worrying about anxiety provoking situations. The main difference between the disorders is that concern about social or performance situations is the main focus in SAD, whereas social or performance concerns are only one of many worries that people with GAD may exhibit. Indeed, the diagnostic criteria for GAD stipulate that individuals worry excessively about a number of life domains, which may include work, school, finances, minor matters, appearance, the future, and world affairs. When making this differential diagnosis, ask these questions (a) Does the person report excessive worry about a number of life domains that are unrelated to social or performance concerns (necessary for a diagnosis of GAD)? (b) If social concerns are one of several excessive worries, are they a large enough problem to stand on their own, regardless of whether criteria for GAD are met)? If the answer to these questions is *yes*, it is possible that the person may have enough symptoms to meet criteria for both disorders. On the other hand, if social concerns are milder, are not accompanied by significant phobic avoidance, and are part of a larger picture of chronic and excessive worry, a diagnosis of GAD may be the most appropriate diagnosis.

Another distinction between these two disorders is that a diagnosis of GAD requires the presence of several physical symptoms including trouble sleeping, muscle tension, and feelings of restlessness. These symptoms are often present in any anxious client, but are not necessary for a diagnosis of SAD.

1.5.3   Specific Phobia

SAD may be confused with certain specific phobias, including fears of crowded or closed-in places (claustrophobia), like a crowded elevator or movie theater, since both of these phobia types may include avoidance of certain public places. To distinguish between SAD and claustrophobia, it is important to ask about the underlying beliefs that are associated with the person's fear. In claustrophobia, the focus of the fear is often focused on the possibility of being unable to breathe or to escape from the situation. In SAD, the focus of the fear is typically on being observed by others, being embarrassed, or humiliated. As with PDA, someone with claustrophobia may report that part of his fear concerns embarrassment about leaving or passing out in front of others. Again, it is important to look at the spectrum of symptoms reported (a broader range of social concerns would be expected in SAD) as well as the proportion of fear attributed to embarrassment versus a physical catastrophe (which would likely be a stronger fear in claustrophobia).

1.5.4   Depression

There are two forms of depression that often have overlapping features with SAD. Major depressive disorder (MDD) is characterized by depressed mood or loss of interest in activities for at least two weeks, accompanied by other symptoms of depression including appetite changes, sleep changes, feelings of worthlessness, low energy, difficulty concentrating, and suicidal ideation or attempts. Dysthymic disorder has many similar symptoms as MDD, but the symptoms are not as severe and are typically more chronic (lasting a minimum of two years). Both forms of depression and SAD may involve withdrawal and avoidance of situations such as going out with friends, socializing, or attending work or school. However, this avoidance is fear-based in SAD and is more often fuelled by low energy and low motivation in depression. In addition, people who experience social withdrawal related to depression typically report feeling comfortable in social situations when they are not feeling depressed.

Another characteristic in common between these disorders is feelings of low self-worth, inadequacy, or even worthlessness. It is not uncommon for individuals with either disorder to report automatic thoughts such as "I can't do this" or "I'll mess up" and also to report beliefs like "I'm inadequate" or "I'm no good." However, depression is more likely than SAD to include thoughts clustering around themes of hopelessness, worthlessness, and helplessness.

Both disorders may involve difficulties concentrating or sleeping. To properly distinguish them, it is important to ask individuals for the reasons behind the presence of these symptoms. For example, why is a person having trouble concentrating or falling asleep? In a depressed presentation, the person might report that she is ruminating about past failures or is feeling guilty about little unimportant omissions. If the presentation is SAD, the individual might be more inclined to report worry about a previous or upcoming social event when trying to sleep.

As is the case for other anxiety disorders, SAD and depression are highly comorbid. Thus, it is likely that both disorders may be present for a given client.

1.5.5   Avoidant Personality Disorder

SAD and avoidant personality disorder share many features, and may actually reflect the same underlying problem

As mentioned earlier, there is significant overlap between SAD and APD, so much so that some have proposed that APD is a severe form of SAD or that both disorders are different ways of labeling a single underlying dimension. DSM-IV-TR defines APD as a pattern of social inhibition and sensitivity to negative evaluation. Both disorders are characterized by this fear of negative evaluation, which leads to significant anxiety and avoidance of social situations. Even though fear and avoidance are present in both disorders, individuals desire social contact and interaction. Both disorders have onsets early in life. Generalized SAD is even harder to distinguish from APD as compared to nongeneralized SAD due to the pervasive nature of symptoms.

Research suggests that individuals with APD may be more interpersonally sensitive than those with SAD and may have poorer social skills (Turner, Beidel, Dancu, & Keys, 1986). Indeed, the degree of interpersonal sensitivity may be a useful way to distinguish these disorders. Whereas individuals with SAD are often sensitive about and fearful of being criticized, this quality appears to be more pervasive and marked in APD. The DSM-IV-TR suggests that people with APD are "preoccupied" with their concern of being criticized. Further, criteria can still be met for SAD even if concerns about being criticized are minimal. Some individuals present with concerns about embarrassing themselves or showing signs of anxiety rather than being criticized by others.

1.5.6   Schizoid Personality Disorder

Schizoid personality disorder is characterized by detachment from and disinterest in social relationships, disinterest in sexual relationships, and few friends or relationships. Individuals with this disorder prefer to be alone and are virtually indifferent to praise or criticism from others. Schizoid personality disorder can appear similar to SAD because of the avoidance of social situations and the lack of close relationships (e.g., both conditions are often associated with avoidance of family gatherings, a lack of intimate relationships, and a tendency to be unmarried). However, there are a number of important distinctions between these disorders. The main distinction to bear in mind is that people with schizoid personality disorder are typically disinterested in social or intimate relationships, whereas people with SAD are often very interested in these relationships, but are simply too anxious to be able to have them. Further, although many people with SAD have small social circles and are not in intimate relationships, a sizeable proportion of them *are* in intimate relationships and report satisfaction with these relationships. Individuals with schizoid personality disorder are rarely involved in these relationships. Another distinction is the range of emotions experienced by individuals. Whereas individuals with schizoid personality disorder have more flat or constrained affect, individuals with SAD have an abundance of anxiety and nervous energy. This difference in affect is often very noticeable during a clinical interview.

1.6   Comorbidity

SAD is associated with an increased risk of a client having another Axis I disorder, including a mood disorder or another anxiety disorder. Brown et al. (2001) found that 46% of people with SAD had another current psychological disorder and that 72% of people with SAD had another psychological disorder in his or her lifetime. More specifically, people with SAD appear to have an increased risk of comorbid panic disorder, specific phobias, and depression. In fact, SAD and posttraumatic stress disorder had the highest rates of comorbid depression out of all the anxiety disorders. A large Canadian study also found that SAD was associated with a moderate level of comorbidity with substance abuse disorders (Chartier, Walker, & Stein, 2003). These higher rates of comorbidity can have an impact on severity of SAD as well as treatment outcome. Clients with SAD who also had an additional diagnosis of depression were found to have a longer duration of SAD symptoms and more severe impairment both before and after treatment than those with a sole diagnosis of SAD (Erwin, Heimberg, Juster, & Mindlin, 2002). In this study, clients with SAD and a comorbid anxiety disorder diagnosis were more similar to those with just SAD on measures of impairment (compared to those with SAD and depression), suggesting that having comorbid depression is more problematic than having a comorbid anxiety disorder. On the other hand, in a different study of individuals with SAD and an additional diagnosis of GAD demonstrated greater symptom severity and impairment than those without GAD (Mennin, Heimberg, & MacAndrew, 2000). It seems likely that the presence of any comorbid disorder can have at least some negative implications for the severity and prognosis of SAD.

Most people with SAD will experience one or more other psychological disorders in their lifetimes

1.7   Diagnostic Procedures and Documentation

Accurate diagnosis of SAD is important for selecting an appropriate treatment. In addition, it is useful to assess the severity of an individual's presentation, the presence of particular features, and the extent to which symptoms changes as a result of treatment. A host of measures exist for assessing these domains, including interviewer administered scales, self-report questionnaires, and behavioral assessments. This section includes an overview of the most commonly used tools for assessing SAD. For a more thorough review of assessment measures, see Antony, Orsillo, and Roemer (2001).

1.7.1   Interviewer Administered Measures

Anxiety Disorders Interview Schedule for DSM-IV (ADIS-IV; Di Nardo, Brown, & Barlow, 1994). The ADIS-IV is a clinician-administered semi-structured interview that provides both diagnostic information and dimensional information (e.g., symptom severity ratings) for a range of psychological problems, including anxiety disorders, mood disorders, somatoform disorders, and substance use disorders. Clinicians require extensive training in the administration of this interview, which can be lengthy (e.g., several hours). Despite these drawbacks for everyday practice, the ADIS-IV has the benefit of providing clear criteria to help determine the presence or absence of SAD (as well as common comorbid disorders) as well as assessing useful information such as the degree of fear and avoidance in a variety of social settings. The ADIS-IV has demonstrated good reliability and validity (e.g., Brown, Di Nardo, Lehman, & Campbell, 2001; Rodebaugh, Heimberg, Woods, Liebowitz, & Schneier, 2006).

> The SCID is a semistructured interview often used to diagnose anxiety disorders (discussed in Chapter 3)

Liebowitz Social Anxiety Scale (LSAS; Liebowitz, 1987). The LSAS is a 24-item clinician-rated scale designed to assess the severity of a range of social and performance concerns. Respondents are asked about both fear and avoidance of a series of situations over the past week, yielding total fear and avoidance scores as well as a number of subscale scores (fear of social interaction, fear of performance, total fear, avoidance of social interaction, avoidance of performance, and total avoidance). Although only a few studies have examined the psychometric properties of the LSAS, it appears to be a reliable and valid measure with good treatment sensitivity (Heimberg et al., 1999). This measure is useful to include in a pre and posttreatment assessment battery as it only takes about 20 minutes to complete and provides a helpful addition to self-reported symptom measures.

Brief Social Phobia Scale (BSPS; Davidson et al., 1991). The BSPS is an 18-item interviewer-rated scale designed to assess the severity of symptoms of SAD. Similar to the LSAS, respondents are asked to rate both fear and avoidance of a number of social situations over the past week. These measures differ in that the BSPS inquires about fewer situations (seven) than the LSAS, but also asks about physiological symptoms that may occur in social situations. The situations assessed include speaking in front of others, talking to people in authority, talking to strangers, being embarrassed or humiliated, being criticized, social gatherings, and doing something while being watched. It is a briefer measure than the LSAS and the ADIS-IV, only taking 5 to 15 minutes to administer, but its authors suggest using it in conjunction with another interview-based measure for thoroughness. Internal consistency for this interview is adequate, and it has demonstrated good validity and treatment sensitivity. It appears that the fear and avoidance subscales of this measure are psychometrically stronger than the physiological subscale, suggesting that these may be the subscales to focus on when assessing treatment outcome (Davidson et al., 1997).

1.7.2   Self-Report Severity Measures

Social Phobia Inventory (SPIN; Connor et al., 2000). This is a 17-item self-report measure assessing how much a series of symptoms of social anxiety bother the respondent. Items fall into three subscales including fear, avoidance, and physiological arousal. Individuals complete the SPIN based on the previous week, making this a useful measure to assess week-to-week progress during treatment for SAD. Another appealing characteristic of the SPIN is its brevity. It takes several minutes to complete, allowing the client to quickly complete it at the beginning of a treatment session. The psychometric properties of the SPIN are very good (Antony, Coons, McCabe, Ashbaugh, & Swinson, 2006; Connor et al., 2000). The total score demonstrates excellent internal consistency, and correlations with interviewer measures of SAD suggest it has good convergent validity. The authors of the SPIN suggest that a cutoff score of 19 (out of a possible 68) is useful in discriminating those with SAD and those without at an accuracy rate of 79%. The SPIN is reproduced in the appendix of this book.

A brief version of SPIN has also been developed

Social Phobia Scale (SPS; Mattick & Clarke, 1998). This is a 20-item self-report scale focusing on anxiety while being observed by others. Respondents rate how much each situation would bother them on a scale from *not at all* to *extremely true of me*. Situations include activities such as using public toilets, entering rooms where others are seated, fainting or being ill in front of others, and eating or drinking in front of others. This is also a brief measure, taking only minutes to complete. This feature makes the SPS a popular measure to use in treatment studies or to monitor weekly progress in treatment. The SPS demonstrates excellent reliability. Even though there are items on the SPS that seem related to agoraphobic concerns (i.e., fears of being ill in front of others), individuals with SAD score higher on this scale than do those with agoraphobia. The SPS has been well-studied and appears to demonstrate strong psychometric properties including treatment sensitivity (see Orsillo, 2001, for a review).

Social Interaction Anxiety Scale (SIAS; Mattick & Clarke, 1998). This self-report measure was designed in conjunction with the SPS and assesses fears of interacting with others. Sample items include concerns about talking with others, mixing at parties, and saying something embarrassing when talking. It contains 19 items and therefore is brief and easy for clients to complete. As with the SPS, it also demonstrates strong psychometric properties and studies suggest that the two measures, though related, are assessing different constructs (Orsillo, 2001).

1.7.3   Behavioral Approach Tests (BATs)

A BAT involves instructing a client to enter a feared situation or engage in a feared activity and monitoring his or her responses (e.g., subjective fear ratings, escape or avoidance, safety behaviors, anxious thoughts, physical sensations, response to changing particular aspects of the situation, etc.). Using behavioral assessment strategies can provide important information not provided by interviews or self-report alone. For example, a client with a tendency to minimize his fears may report little or no avoidance of a particular situation, but then may freeze when in the actual situation. BATs can also be used to assess treatment outcome. A change in performance on a behavioral task provides real-world information about the effectiveness of treatment.

A commonly used BAT for SAD involves asking a client to give a speech in front of another person, a small audience, or a video camera. This situation is often used because public speaking is one of the most common fears that adults report, suggesting that it is likely to be anxiety-provoking for most individuals, especially those with a diagnosis of SAD. Other examples of BATs include having the individual engage in a spontaneous conversation or talk about himself to others. Although it is sometimes useful to have all participants engage in a consistent BAT for the purpose of research, it is typically more appropriate to use individually tailored BATs in clinical practice, selecting situations that are most relevant to the individual's phobia and treatment goals.

When designing a BAT, the clinician and client should identify a highly feared situation (ideally, one of the most feared situations) and then have the client enter that situation both before and after treatment (and perhaps several times during the course of treatment). During the BAT, clients should provide subjective fear ratings to communicate their distress, using a scale ranging from 0 (*no fear at all*) to 100 (*as much fear as can be imagined*). Other scales (e.g., 0 to 10) are fine as well. In addition to subjective fear ratings, other indicators of fear can be useful as well, including whether the client can complete the BAT, how long he or she spends in the situation, and objective signs of anxiety (e.g., shaking, trouble concentrating on questions, etc.).

1.7.4   Assessing Suitability for Treatment

As clinicians, we often assume that people are ready to engage in whatever treatment we have to offer when they present in a clinical setting. We also know that CBT is an effective treatment for SAD, so we may assume that this approach is always a good match for a client who presents to us with this problem. However, full benefit from a treatment like CBT depends on the active participation of clients. Clients have to be willing to "buy into" the cognitive behavioral model of social anxiety and practice the CBT techniques. Homework is a crucial part of successful outcome in CBT, requiring the client to not only attend appointments, but also to practice using techniques and completing exercises between sessions. However, many clients are not fully ready to commit to CBT, or may be ambivalent about engaging in treatment. It is helpful to know which clients are ready to begin active treatment, which clients are almost ready, and which clients are not likely to benefit from treatment at the current time. Knowing this information is useful not only for the clinician (i.e., it reduces the amount of time spent with clients who are not ready, it reduces the likelihood of frustration from working with a "resistant" client), but also for the client who might feel frustrated or hopeless about trying and "failing" a therapy that he or she was not ready to do. For these reasons, it can be helpful to assess suitability and readiness for CBT.

To briefly assess suitability for CBT for SAD, consider the following areas. First, what is the client's reaction to the CBT model? Do clients believe that their anxiety has a psychological component, or do they firmly believe that anxiety is physiologically based? Do they understand the detrimental role that avoidance plays in maintaining anxiety? Can they access examples of anxiety-provoking thoughts? Are they willing to experience temporary increases in anxiety and fear in order to eventually feel more comfortable in social situations?

Furthermore, are clients comfortable with the structure and style of CBT? CBT for social anxiety is present-focused, so clients who are looking to examine the developmental or unconscious "roots" of their anxiety may not appreciate a problem-focused approach such as CBT. Do clients indicate a willingness to complete homework? Do they understand the crucial role that between-session work has on treatment outcome? It is useful to ask about previous attempts at therapy, including CBT and other techniques. How did the client react to previous therapies? Was he or she able to do the "work" required by previous therapists? Clinicians could also investigate the relative strength of the client's fear of engaging in treatment (e.g., completing exposures, confronting anxiety) versus the costs and frustrations of living with anxiety.

Note that there is little research on whether suitability for CBT can be reliably assessed and whether assessing suitability for CBT leads to better outcomes. Furthermore, there are no standardized assessments for suitability for CBT in SAD. However, the interested reader is referred to Safran and Segal (1996) for a thorough overview of a standard suitability interview for cognitive therapy of depression. Note that this interview is more focused on cognitive strategies than behavioral strategies, and that its reliability and validity are not well studied.

2

Psychological Approaches to Understanding Social Anxiety Disorder

Although classification schemes such as the DSM-IV-TR (American Psychiatric Association, 2000) provide thorough *descriptions* of psychological disorders, they do not aid in understanding how these disorders begin or are maintained. However, there are a number of psychological models and theories of the development and maintenance of SAD. This chapter discusses several of the most influential of these models. The first two approaches (Clark & Wells, 1995; Rapee & Heimberg, 1997) describe the process of social anxiety from a cognitive-behavioral perspective. Generally, these and other cognitive behavioral models suggest that SAD stems from a tendency to misinterpret social situations as dangerous and to engage in safety and avoidance behaviors that help to maintain the fear and anxiety over time. The chapter also reviews the roles of negative learning experiences and temperament in the development of SAD.

> Cognitive models of SAD hypothesize that social anxiety stems from a tendency to interpret social situations as being dangerous or threatening

2.1   The Cognitive Model of Clark and Wells

Clark and Wells (1995) proposed a cognitive model of SAD based on their clinical observations and research. Their model begins with the assumption that people with SAD are invested in making a positive impression on others, but are insecure about their ability to do so. These insecurities likely arise from distorted beliefs that people with SAD hold about themselves. Common negative beliefs in SAD include "I'm stupid" or "I'm boring." People with SAD also hold negative assumptions about themselves and others (e.g., "If I'm quiet people will think I'm boring" and "If people see my anxiety they'll think I'm stupid") and rigid rules about how they should behave in social situations (e.g., "I should never show signs of anxiety" or "I should always have something interesting to say"). Table 1 provides additional examples of negative beliefs, assumptions, and rules often associated with SAD. Clearly, holding strong and negative ideas such as these about oneself and about how one should perform in social situations can leave a person vulnerable to experiencing high levels of anxiety in these situations.

According to this model, people with SAD also have a tendency to focus on *themselves* in social situations rather than attending to what others are saying and doing. In some ways, this is contradictory with what we might expect – we might assume that people with SAD would be constantly monitoring how others are reacting to them and whether others seem to like them, accept them, etc. However, Clark and Wells suggest that attention becomes self-focused, to

Table 1
Examples of Beliefs, Assumptions, and Rules in Social Anxiety Disorder

Beliefs	• I'm stupid.
	• I'm incompetent.
	• I'm boring.
	• I'm weird, odd, or different.
Assumptions	• If I make a mistake, others will think I'm stupid.
	• If other people notice my anxiety, they'll think I'm a failure.
	• If I mess up what I'm saying, no one will listen to me.
	• If one person doesn't like me, no one will like me.
Rules	• Everyone should like me.
	• I should never show that I'm nervous.
	• I should always look "perfect."
	• I should always sound intelligent and interesting.
	• I should always have something interesting to say.

the point that the individual might ignore or miss important social cues (e.g., signs of being liked, a person nodding in agreement). Self-focused attention is promoted by the increase in physiological symptoms a person experiences when anticipating or entering a social situation. In other words, as the person becomes more anxious, bodily sensations intensify (e.g., increased heart rate, sweating, shaking), and these sensations cause a shift in attention to oneself and one's body. The ultimate result of self-focused attention is an increased feeling of conspicuousness. The person feels like he or she is "on stage" or the "center of attention." Individuals with SAD may even see themselves as if they are watching themselves on television. One client said to us that he felt so hot and sweaty that he had an image of himself with a bright red and sweaty face "like a tomato." In reality, this may not have been the true state of affairs (actual blushing, as rated by independent observers, is often not related to an individual's belief that he or she is blushing; Mulkens, de Jong, Dobbelaar, and Bögels, 1999), but such an impression served to exacerbate anxiety and reduce the person's ability to attend to normal social feedback.

The host of negative beliefs people with SAD hold may also cause them to behave differently than nonanxious people in stressful situations. Clark and Wells call some of these behaviors "safety behaviors." Safety behaviors are those that help the person avoid a feared catastrophe and feel safer in a particular situation. Examples of safety behaviors can be found in Table 2.

Another common strategy used by people with SAD is avoidance of a stressful situation. Both safety behaviors and avoidance are completely understandable. Who would want to put themselves in a highly stressful situation? However, Clark and Wells point out that avoidance and safety behaviors lead to a number of problems. First, some safety behaviors may actually exacerbate feared bodily sensations. For example, wearing an extra jacket to hide any sweating actually makes a person warmer and therefore more likely to sweat. Rehearsing questions and answers in one's mind during a conversation actually takes attention away from the conversation, making it more difficult to be a part of the discourse. As discussed earlier, Clark and Wells argue that

People with SAD often use safety behaviors to reduce anxiety or protect themselves from perceived danger in social situations

Table 2
Examples of Safety Behaviors in Social Anxiety Disorder

- Overly rehearse what I'm going to say in a conversation; prepare questions in advance.
- Sit in the back row of a class or in the corner of the meeting room.
- Wear a turtleneck sweater to hide blushing and splotches on my neck and chest.
- Bring my spouse or a friend with me.
- Memorize my speech.
- Wear cool clothes to avoid sweating, or a jacket over my shirt to hide my sweating.
- Eat in a dimly lit restaurant to prevent people from noticing my blushing.
- Grip my water bottle very tightly to prevent hands from shaking.
- Always be perfectly dressed and made up before going out.

the bodily sensations of anxiety cause an unhelpful shift in attention to one's internal state, preventing the individual from focusing on important events in his or her surroundings. Another problem associated with avoidance and safety behaviors is the prevention of any opportunity to learn that negative outcomes typically do not occur. For example, by not ever giving a speech, a person can never learn that he may be perfectly capable of public speaking or that the audience is much less likely to be critical or dismissing than anticipated. Using safety behaviors gives the person a ready-made excuse for why a catastrophe did not happen (e.g., "it was because I prevented it by using my safety behavior"). Clark and Wells describe a third problem with using these coping strategies, namely that safety and avoidance behaviors contain their own messages to others that may be more damaging than the person's original fear. For example, if a person is afraid of not having anything to say in a conversation, he may rehearse questions and answers in his head while the other person talks (a safety behavior). Although this behavior is intended to *help* the conversation, it may actually *hurt* the conversation. This individual may come off as disinterested, aloof, or disengaged from the conversation, actually *increasing* his chance of being socially "rejected." Avoidance, as well, can be associated with negative consequences. By repeatedly declining social invitations, the person's friends may grow tired of continually asking but being rejected. By repeatedly avoiding things like meetings, work events, etc., a person may be putting herself in jeopardy of being fired or not considered for promotions. Safety behaviors and avoidance are important components of a feedback cycle that contributes to the maintenance of negative beliefs about the self and negative predictions about what will happen if the person were to enter a feared situation. With these negative beliefs and predications intact and perhaps strengthened, anxiety symptoms are maintained.

The final piece of the Clark and Wells model involves the notion that negative beliefs, rules, and predictions do not just occur when the person is in the feared situation. Indeed, negative processing is theorized to occur

Table 3
Summary of Key Points from the Clark and Wells Model of Social Anxiety Disorder

- People with SAD *want* to make a good impression on others.
- They hold negative beliefs about themselves and their ability to perform in social situations.
- When in social situations, people with SAD focus on themselves and see themselves as if they're watching themselves on television.
- Focusing on themselves doesn't allow people with SAD to fully participate in the social situation.
- People with SAD either avoid situations or use safety behaviors in feared situations.
- Safety behaviors and avoidance do not allow the person to learn that fears may not actually come true.
- Negative thinking about social situations occurs before, during, and after exposure to the situation.

before the person even enters a feared situation ("anticipatory processing"). The person might review all the terrible things that could happen, how he or she may "screw up," and how badly things have gone in the past. This type of processing will either cause the person to completely avoid the situation, or enter the situation in an already self-focused, negative mindset. After making it through a difficult situation, people with SAD also have a tendency to review how things went (what Clark and Wells refer to as the "postmortem"). Unfortunately, for all the reasons described earlier, the situation may not have gone well or the person with SAD may have disregarded any positive or neutral feedback, meaning that the postmortem review will only serve to consolidate negative beliefs.

A summary of the key points from the Clark and Wells model of SAD is provided in Table 3.

2.2   The Cognitive Behavioral Model of Rapee and Heimberg

Rapee and Heimberg (1997) have also described a cognitive behavioral model of SAD that shares many features with the model by Clark and Wells but also contains some unique ideas. Both models share the notion that people with SAD hold negative beliefs about themselves and are likely to predict that bad things will happen in stressful situations. In other words, both models emphasize distorted information processing in SAD. Further, the occurrence of negative evaluation by others is seen as being "catastrophic," making it a highly undesirable outcome. Both models discuss the unhelpful nature of avoidance and subtle avoidance (or safety behaviors), suggesting that they can actually contribute to worse outcomes even though they are used to help a person get through a stressful situation.

According to Rapee and Heimberg, a source of perceived threat for people with SAD is the belief that others hold unreasonably high expectations of them

Rapee and Heimberg explicitly discuss the notion that the perceived threat in SAD is the reaction of an "audience." By audience, they are referring to any person who may perceive or notice an individual. Thus, if there is no perceived audience, social anxiety is unlikely to exist. However, because most social or performance situations include at least a possible audience (e.g., even walking down the street involves an audience of other people who are also on the street, drivers in cars, people looking out windows, etc.), the person with SAD is likely to feel anxious in many social situations. As a result of being concerned about an audience reaction, people with SAD create a mental representation of how they look or appear to this audience. This mental representation is influenced by a number of sources including a self-image from memory, pictures, physical symptoms, and social feedback. Note that the influence of physical sensations on self-image is also seen in the Clark and Wells model, but the actual type of representation remains distinct. Clark and Wells suggest the person sees himself as though he is on television, whereas Rapee and Heimberg describe the self-image as a mental representation. This mental image of oneself is often distorted. For example, people with SAD often rate their performance as poor, even if this is not objectively true. Indeed, some research has found that the performance of people with SAD is not objectively different than people who do not have anxiety (e.g., Rapee & Lim, 1992), though other studies have found some deficits in the social performance of individuals with SAD, including children (Spence, Donovan, & Brechman-Toussaint, 1999). Rapee and Heimberg argue that anxiety may sometimes interfere with performance, leading to objective evidence that one is "incapable" or a "failure."

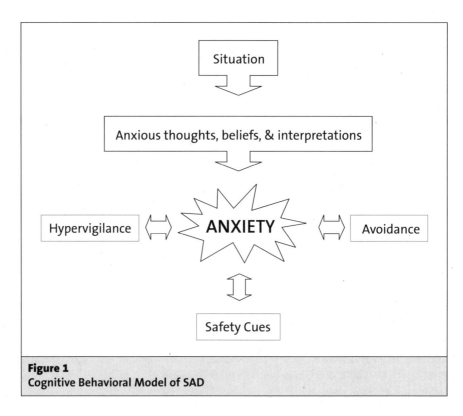

Figure 1
Cognitive Behavioral Model of SAD

Not only do people with SAD monitor their mental representation of themselves, but they also pay a great deal of attention to looking for sources of "threat." Threat usually comes in the form of being negatively evaluated by others, so the person with SAD looks for signs of rejection, disinterest, or embarrassment. Unfortunately, it is often hard to tell what others are thinking, and it is rare to receive straightforward feedback about one's performance (e.g., "you are a decent conversationalist" or "I wasn't paying attention in the meeting because I was thinking about my wife, not because you were boring"). Therefore, it is easy to distort or twist social information to be consistent with one's fears. Someone yawning during a talk is easily interpreted as a sign of the speaker being boring, and the person yawning is easily picked out of a crowd of neutral faces when a great deal of attention is allocated to signs of threat.

Similar across both models is the notion that feedback loops exist to maintain social anxiety and maintain distorted predictions and beliefs about self and others. See Figure 1 for a visual representation of the feedback loops. For example, perceptions of oneself as awkward or unable to carry on a conversation will lead to heightened anxiety when there is a perceived audience. This heightened anxiety leads to an increase in bodily sensations, which strengthens one's self-perceptions of being awkward and appearing anxious. As a result, individuals may be inclined to leave the stressful situation, or to avoid it altogether, not allowing them to test out their assumptions of what would happen if they stayed despite their anxiety.

2.3   Negative Learning Experiences and Social Anxiety

Models that include negative learning experiences in the etiology of fear have applications for understanding the development of SAD. Rachman (1977) highlighted three pathways to the development of fears. These pathways include (a) *direct conditioning*, which refers to a stimulus becoming associated with a fear reaction though a traumatic experience, (b) *vicarious acquisition*, which involves witnessing someone else have a fearful reaction or upsetting social experience, and (c) *informational pathways*, which involve learning that a particular stimulus (i.e., social situations) is dangerous through information transmitted by others (e.g., on television, during conversations, while reading, etc.).

There is some evidence for the presence of these pathways to fear in SAD. For example, retrospective reports of individuals with SAD suggest that they experienced more teasing in childhood than did individuals with obsessive compulsive disorder or panic disorder (McCabe, Antony, Summerfeldt, Liss, & Swinson, 2003), reports of severe bullying during childhood were related to a higher frequency of SAD in clients presenting to an outpatient depression clinic (Gladstone, Parker, & Malhi, 2006), and reports of being frequently teased during childhood were related to scores on measures of social anxiety in college students (Roth, Coles, & Heimberg, 2002). Further, several studies have found that socially anxious individuals are often raised by socially isolated parents, and that parents may hold these children and adolescents back

There is tendency for people with SAD to report a history of childhood teasing more often than people without SAD

from social experiences (e.g., Bögels, van Oosten, Muris, & Smulders, 2001). This kind of evidence can be construed as potential sources of both vicarious acquisition (e.g., watching a parent act in an anxious, withdrawn manner) and/ or informational learning (e.g., being instructed by anxious parents that social outings are dangerous). In observational studies, parents of anxious children appear to be more likely than other parents to support their children's desires to be avoidant (Dadds, Barrett, Rapee, & Ryan, 1996). Finally, a study by Öst and Hugdahl (1981) found that 13% of individuals with SAD reported that vicarious learning experiences played a role in the development of their symptoms.

Although there is some evidence suggesting that negative learning experiences may play a role in the development of SAD, they cannot fully explain how SAD develops. Many people with SAD cannot recall traumatic experiences and grew up in sociable environments. Similarly, many people who do not develop symptoms of SAD can recall adverse childhood experiences like being teased. Therefore, negative learning experiences are just one potential pathway to the development of this disorder.

2.4   Temperamental Bases of SAD

Some authors have been interested in the temperamental and developmental precursors to SAD. Are some people simply born with SAD? The answer to this appears to be that some people are born with a *vulnerability* to developing SAD. No one gene can explain the development of SAD – anxiety disorders are too complex to be controlled by single genes. Similarly, not every child born to a parent with SAD will develop this disorder and not every individual with SAD has an afflicted parent, though SAD tends to aggregate within families, suggesting some genetic component as well as environmental influences. Several twin studies suggest a significant but moderate genetic influence in the development of SAD and social anxiety (Kendler, Neale, Kessler, Heath, & Eaves, 1992; Stein, Jang, & Livesley, 2002) and it appears that the genetic risk for the anxiety disorders, including SAD, is best understood as inheriting risk for one of a cluster of anxiety disorders rather than a particular disorder (Hettema, Prescott, Myers, Neale, & Kendler, 2005).

Thus, it appears that the role of temperament is important to understand. The temperamental vulnerability most often linked with social anxiety is called *behavioral inhibition*. Behavioral inhibition involves a tendency to overreact to novel environmental stimuli in social domains and is thought to have a genetic basis. In other words, a child demonstrating behavioral inhibition will show physiological reactivity, shyness, and possible withdrawal when faced with a new situation (e.g., clinging to one's parent when meeting a new adult, not being interested in playing with new children or new toys, being less likely to initiate an interaction with another child). Studies have found a relationship between behavioral inhibition in childhood and the development of social anxiety in adolescence or adulthood when these inhibited children are followed across time (Hirshfeld-Becker et al., 2003). This link is especially strong for children whose signs of inhibition were consistent across multiple

Behavioral inhibition in infancy is predictive of later developing an anxiety disorder, such as SAD

testing situations (i.e., when behavioral inhibition appears in a number of situations, not just in isolated incidents).

Although behavioral inhibition appears to be fairly stable across time, especially among individuals with extreme levels of behavioral inhibition, there is some variability in this construct across time. Some authors have argued that this suggests that family and peer interactions also influence levels of social anxiety (Neal & Edelmann, 2003). Indeed, the interaction of a temperamental style with environment is an intuitively meaningful way to understand the development of SAD. An inhibited child will be more likely to "pull" for overprotective behaviors from his or her parent, which then reduces the child's opportunities to get used to novel situations, thus strengthening the inhibition. Studies suggest that parents of inhibited and shy children may be more overprotective, intrusive, insensitive, and shaming (Hudson & Rapee, 2001; Klonsky, Dutton, & Liebel, 1990). As children begin to interact with peers, research suggests that initial shyness or passivity is tolerated until adolescence, but then results in rejection (Blöte & Westenberg, 2007; Rubin & Mills, 1988). Supporting this notion is research that suggests individuals with social anxiety were teased in childhood and adolescence more than individuals with other anxiety disorders (McCabe et al., 2003). Thus Neal and Edelmann (2003) suggest that the style a child is born with (that is, behavioral inhibition) strongly interacts with family and peer influences to create a vulnerability to the development of SAD.

2.5   Implications for Treatment

The models described in this chapter have implications for the treatment of SAD. Cognitive behavioral treatments (CBT; see Chapter 4), focus on helping a to person gain a more realistic perspective on his or her negative beliefs, assumptions, and rules. Clients are asked to consider the evidence for their anxious beliefs and to actively test their assumptions in order to come to realistic conclusions about the likely outcome of social events. CBT also focuses on changing the coping strategies used by people with SAD. The use of avoidance and safety behaviors are gradually reduced, allowing the person to actually find out what actually happens in these situations and to learn to cope with any untoward outcomes or high levels of anxiety. Techniques such as video feedback may be used to help pull the person's focus of attention from *internal* cues to *external* social cues. Given the relationships among thoughts, emotions, and coping strategies, a focus on any one of these areas should help shift the entire system. For example, by learning to think more realistically, people may find that the need to use safety behaviors is reduced. Similarly, by entering feared situations, they will obtain new information that may be useful for understanding the *realistic* consequences of being in these situations.

3

Diagnosis and Treatment Indications

This chapter provides the clinician with a framework for understanding a client's SAD, and for selecting an appropriate course of treatment. It begins with a discussion of key features to be assessed, followed by an overview of effective treatment strategies, and guidelines for how to use information from the assessment to plan for treatment.

3.1   Key Features to be Assessed

Key features that should be assessed include situational triggers, physical features, cognitive features, avoidance strategies, safety behaviors, anxiety sensitivity, social skills, environmental factors, comorbidity, and degree of impairment. The extent to which these various features are present in any given client will influence the types of strategies that are used, and the ways in which they are implemented. This discussion also includes recommended instruments that can be used to aid assessment. Many of these instruments are reviewed and reprinted in the *Practitioner's Guide to Empirically-Based Measures of Anxiety* (Antony et al., 2001), and several are discussed in more detail in Chapter 1.

3.1.1   Situational Triggers

Cognitive behavioral therapy (CBT) depends on being able to identify situations that trigger an individual's fear. In the case of SAD, these include performance situations in which an individual might be the center of attention (e.g., public speaking, eating or drinking in front of others, speaking in meetings, walking down the street), as well as interpersonal or social situations (e.g., conversations, dating, being assertive, meeting strangers, interviews). The clinician should generate a comprehensive list of the client's feared situations. This list of situations is used for creating an exposure hierarchy, and for selecting situations for exposure practices.

Scales that can be useful for generating a list of situational triggers include self report measures such as the Social Phobia Inventory (Connor et al., 2000), Social Phobia Scale (Mattick & Clarke, 1998), and Social Interaction Anxiety Inventory (Mattick & Clarke, 1998), as well as clinician administered skills such as the Brief Social Phobia Scale (BSPS; Davidson et al., 1991) and Liebowitz Social Anxiety Scale (LSAS; Liebowitz, 1987). Chapter 1 includes detailed descriptions of these scales.

3.1.2   Physical Features

People with SAD often experience panic attacks in the presence of the situations that they fear. A panic attack is a rush of fear and that peaks in 10 minutes or less, and includes four or more symptoms from the following list: racing or pounding heart, sweating, trembling or shaking, shortness of breath, choking feelings, tightness or discomfort in the chest, nausea or abdominal distress, dizziness or faintness, feeling unreal or detached, numbness or tingling sensations, hot flushes or chills, fear of dying, and fear of losing control or going "crazy." Symptoms of autonomic arousal (e.g., increased heart rate) are particularly common in performance related fears. For example, individuals who fear public speaking are more likely to experience a racing and pounding heart in their feared situations than are individuals who fear a wide range of social situations (Levin et al., 1993). Individuals with SAD tend to be most concerned about physical sensations that might be noticeable to others, such as blushing, shaking, and sweating. However, it is important to note that a person's beliefs about the intensity of these symptoms are not necessarily related to the actual intensity of these symptoms. For example, Mulkens et al. (1999) found that although individuals who were fearful of blushing did not blush more than nonfearful individuals during socially stressful challenges (based on ratings by independent judges), the fearful participants were significantly more likely than nonfearful participants to report significant blushing during the challenge.

Individuals with SAD may overestimate the extent to which their symptoms are noticeable to others

An instrument that measures the severity of these types of physical sensations, as well as the individual's concern over experiencing these symptoms is the Blushing, Trembling, and Sweating Questionnaire (Bögels & Reith, 1999), which has been translated into English from the original Dutch version. For individuals who are concerned about experiencing particular physical symptoms, it may be useful to include treatment strategies that target the fear of sensations (see Section 3.1.6 on Anxiety Sensitivity).

3.1.3   Cognitive Features

A thorough assessment of anxiety-provoking thoughts and predictions is essential in planning for a course of CBT. Chapter 2 (Table 1) includes examples of beliefs, assumptions, and rules that often contribute to social anxiety. Questions that may be useful for assessing the cognitive features of social anxiety include:

The focus of assessment should be on identifying specific predictions that the client is making with respect to social situations

- What do you imagine will happen when you _____ (name situation)?
- What might occur if people were to notice your _____ (name symptom)?
- What might people think of you if you were to _____ (name feared outcome)?
- What is your most feared outcome when you think about doing _____ (name situation)?
- What would be so bad about doing _____ in front of others?

- What would be so bad about people thinking _____ about you?
- What would it mean about you if others were to think _____ about you?
- Do you fear that others will think you are stupid? Incompetent? Boring? Rude? Anxious? Weak? Silly? Foolish?

Note that each of these questions is designed to assess an anxiety provoking belief about something that might happen in the future in a social or performance situation (e.g., what might happen if you were to make a mistake in front of others?), or to assess the client's beliefs about the meaning of possible events (e.g., what would it mean about if you were to blush in front of others?). A thorough assessment of the cognitive features of SAD should occur before the start of treatment, though the process should continue throughout therapy as well. In addition to the clinical interview, the cognitive features of SAD may also be assessed using self-report scales such as the Social Thoughts and Beliefs Scale (STABS; Turner, Johnson, Beidel, Heiser, & Lydiard, 2003) and the Speech Anxiety Thoughts Questionnaire (SATI; Cho, Smits, & Telch, 2004).

3.1.4   Avoidance Strategies

The most obvious forms of avoidance in SAD include refusal to enter a feared situation (e.g., avoiding taking courses that involve making a presentation) and escape from a feared situation shortly after entering (e.g., leaving a party after 15 minutes). A complete list of situations that are avoided is important for assessing the severity of SAD and for developing appropriate exposure exercises. In most cases, the list of avoided situations will be similar to the list of situational triggers for social anxiety as discussed in Section 3.1.1. The assessment tools mentioned in that section are all useful for developing a list of avoided situations.

> **Subtle avoidance strategies are commonly used by people with SAD to decrease anxiety or perceived danger associated with a social situation**

Most people with SAD will also use more subtle avoidance strategies to manage the intensity of their anxiety and fear when in social situations, and to prevent their feared consequences from occurring. These strategies are discussed in Section 3.1.5, under the heading of safety behaviors.

3.1.5   Safety Behaviors

Safety behaviors are behaviors that clients use to protect themselves from feeling overly anxious or to prevent their feared consequences from actually occurring. Examples of safety behaviors include:

- Wearing extra make-up or a turtleneck sweater to hide blushing on the face or neck.
- Avoiding activities in public that might increase flushing in the face or sweating (e.g., exercise, eating hot foods, drinking alcohol, wearing warm clothing).
- Over-preparing for presentations, meetings, or other social situations (e.g., memorizing a presentation or trying to anticipate all questions that may arise during a meeting).

- Drinking alcohol or using other drugs before entering feared situations.
- Always bringing a companion when entering a feared situation.
- Steering conversations toward "safe" topics (e.g., avoiding talking about oneself by repeatedly asking another individual questions).
- Selecting positions (e.g., when standing in a room or sitting at a table) to minimize interactions with others.
- Taking on "roles" in social situations to minimize interactions with others (e.g., offering to serve food or do dishes at a family function).
- Ensuring that lights are dimmed at parties, at restaurants, etc.
- Averting eye contact in an effort to avoid being noticed by others.
- Distracting oneself from anxiety provoking sensations.

There is evidence that among individuals with SAD, safety behaviors contribute to impairment in social performance (Stangier, Heidenreich, & Schermelleh-Engel, 2006) and that overuse of safety behaviors can interfere with the outcome of psychological treatment for SAD (Kim, 2005; Morgan & Raffle, 1999). Therefore, reduction of safety behaviors is an important goal of treatment. The Social Phobia Safety Behaviors Scale (Pinto-Gouveia, Cunha, & do Céo Salvador, 2003) is an example of a scale designed to measure safety behaviors in this population.

3.1.6   Anxiety Sensitivity

Anxiety sensitivity refers to anxiety over experiencing physical symptoms of anxiety, such as elevated heart rate, dizziness, shaking, shortness of breath, etc. Although anxiety sensitivity is particularly elevated in panic disorder, it has been found to be heightened in a wide range of other anxiety problems, including SAD (Taylor et al., 1992). Moreover, people with SAD tend to be particularly concerned about experiencing observable anxiety reactions (e.g., blushing, shaking, sweating), compared to people with other anxiety disorders (Deacon & Abramowitz, 2006). Unlike individuals with panic disorder who are fearful of experiencing physical sensations of arousal across a wide range of situations, people with SAD are generally more likely to fear these sensations only in social or performance-related situations.

> **People with SAD often have elevated levels of anxiety sensitivity, or anxiety over experiencing symptoms of arousal and fear**

The most extensively studied measure for assessing anxiety sensitivity is the Anxiety Sensitivity Index (ASI; Peterson & Reiss, 1993). There are a number of unofficial revisions of the ASI available, the most popular of which is Taylor and Cox's (1998) 36-item version. As reviewed earlier, the Blushing, Trembling, and Sweating Questionnaire (Bögels & Reith, 1999) can also be used to measure concern over experiencing these three particular sensations.

3.1.7   Social Skills

In many cases, cognitive behavioral treatment assumes that the main problem in SAD is an individual's belief that he or she is likely to behave in a socially unacceptable way, rather than a true impairment in social skills.

Often social skills improve naturally as the individual's anxiety improves during treatment

Nevertheless, there is evidence that some individuals with SAD do have greater social skills impairment (e.g., poor eye contact, impaired conversation flow, visible signs of anxiety), relative to people without SAD (Fydrich, Chambless, Perry, Buergener, & Beazley, 1998). For many individuals, treatment is effective regardless of whether social skills are targeted directly. However, in clients with severe social skills deficits, it may be helpful to include social skills training as a component of treatment. There are no empirically supported self-report scales for measuring social skills impairment in people with SAD. In clinical settings, social skills impairment is typically assessed through behavioral observation and information derived from the clinical interview.

3.1.8   Environmental Factors

It is important to assess variables in the client's environment that may be contributing to his or her social anxiety. For example, clients may have people in their lives (e.g., family members, friends, colleagues, or a boss) who contribute to their anxiety by criticizing their behavior unnecessarily. Other clients may have individuals in their social circles who reinforce avoidance behaviors by encouraging them to avoid situations that trigger discomfort, or by offering to do things for the client so that he or she does not have to confront feared situations. Finally, clients may have lifestyles that provide few opportunities for social interaction. For example, in the case of a client who has no relationship, no friends, and no job, it may be necessary to find ways to increase the client's social contacts in order to provide opportunities in which he or she can practice cognitive behavioral treatment strategies. Environmental factors that contribute to a client's social anxiety, or that may prevent the client from overcoming his or her social anxiety, are typically assessed during the course of a comprehensive clinical interview.

It may be necessary to address circumstances in the client's environment that contribute to his or her anxiety

3.1.9   Comorbidity

It is important to assess the degree of comorbidity, the relative severity of each comorbid condition, and whether comorbid problems are likely to interfere with the treatment of SAD (e.g., severe depression or substance dependence may require treatment before social anxiety symptoms can be effectively targeted). A number of instruments exist for assessing comorbidity and anxiety disorders. The best researched of these are semistructured clinician-administered interviews such as the Anxiety Disorders Interview Schedule for DSM-IV (ADIS-IV; Di Nardo, Brown, & Barlow, 1994) and the Structured Clinical Interview for DSM-IV (SCID-IV; First, Spitzer, Gibbon, & Williams, 1996). In addition, the Psychiatric Diagnostic Screening Questionnaire (PDSQ; Zimmerman & Mattia, 2001) is a self-report scale that screens for 13 different DSM-IV Axis I categories, and preliminary data on the psychometric properties of this scale are promising.

3.1.10   Functional Impairment

Assessing impairment in functioning is important for several reasons. First the degree of functional impairment associated with particular aspects of an individual's SAD may influence the target behaviors selected for treatment. For example, a man who fears public speaking, but who experiences no distress or impairment associated with his fear because he has no interest or need to speak in front of groups, will likely not require treatment for this particular fear. However, the same individual may require treatment for his fear of dating if his inability to speak comfortably with women is impairing and if being in a relationship is one of his goals for therapy.

A second reason for carefully assessing functional impairment is to determine whether interference with functioning is so severe that it needs to be targeted directly during the treatment. For example if a client's social anxiety has prevented her from ever being in a relationship or holding a job, she may require additional treatment focused on these areas, including vocational counseling and therapy that provides her with the necessary skills to facilitate the development of new relationships.

A number of brief questionnaires are available for measuring functional impairment. One example is the Illness Intrusiveness Ratings Scale (IIRS; Devins et al., 1983), which assesses impairment in 13 different life domains (e.g., work, social relationships, recreation, financial situation, health, etc.). Research with the IIRS has found impairment in SAD to be significant across most life domains, but particularly high with respect to functioning in social relationships and self-expression and improvement (Antony et al., 1998).

3.2   Overview of Effective Treatment Strategies

The most frequently studied, evidence-based, psychological strategies for treating SAD include (a) cognitive strategies, (b) exposure-based strategies, and (c) social skills training. Each of these is described in Table 4. In addition, there are some studies suggesting that applied relaxation (involving progressive muscle relaxation combined with exposure) is also useful (for a review, see Rodebaugh, Holaway, & Heimberg, 2004).

Evidence-based psychological treatments for SAD usually include various combinations of cognitive strategies, exposure, and social skills training, collectively referred to as cognitive behavioral therapy (CBT). Studies investigating which of these components are necessary for effective treatment have yielded mixed results. For example, whereas some studies have found that the combination of exposure plus cognitive therapy works better than exposure alone, other studies have found exposure alone to be just as effective as the combination (see Rodebaugh et al., 2004). Similarly, whereas some studies have found that social skills training can improve upon the effectiveness of CBT without social skills training (Herbert et al., 2005), numerous studies have found that treatment without explicit social skills training is usually quite effective (Rodebaugh et al., 2004).

Studies comparing CBT to supportive psychotherapies for SAD have generally found CBT to be superior

Table 4
Evidence-Based Psychological Strategies for Treating Social Anxiety Disorder

Treatment Strategy	Description
Cognitive therapy	• Involves learning to identify anxiety provoking thoughts (e.g., I will make a fool of myself during a presentation), and to replace such thoughts with more realistic thoughts and predictions, after examining the evidence. • Clients complete thought records on which they record (a) their initial thoughts, (b) the evidence for and against their initial beliefs or other alternatives for their initial beliefs, and (c) their new beliefs based on their review of the evidence. • Clients carry out behavioral experiments to test out the validity of their anxious thoughts and predictions.
Exposure therapy	• Involves confronting anxiety provoking situations directly until they no longer trigger fear and anxiety. • Typically, exposure begins with entering easier situations on the client's hierarchy first and gradually working up to entering more challenging situations. • Exposure practices include confronting feared social situations in real life, as well as engaging in simulated exposures or role-plays. • For clients who fear physical sensations of anxiety, interoceptive exposure (i.e., symptom exposure) may be used (e.g., exercising to become sweaty before entering a social situation).
Social skills training	• Involves learning to improve social and communication skills through a process of education, rehearsal, and feedback. • Behaviors that may be addressed through social skills training include eye contact, body language, strategies for making small talk, presentation skills, assertiveness skills, teaching skills, strategies for managing conflict, listening skills, and others. • Social skills training is often conducted in the context of behavioral rehearsal, both in real social situations and through role-play practices.

There is no consistent evidence that combining CBT and medication leads to better outcomes than either approach alone for SAD treatment

In addition to psychosocial approaches for treating SAD, there is considerable evidence supporting pharmacological treatments for anxiety disorders, including a variety of antidepressants, anxiolytics, and other medications (Swinson et al., 2006). Medications with support from at least one randomized controlled trial are listed in Table 5. Note that relapse rates tend to be higher following discontinuation of pharmacotherapy then for discontinuation of cognitive behavioral therapy (Liebowitz et al., 1999). In the most comprehensive study to date on the combination of pharmacotherapy (fluoxetine) and CBT for SAD, there was no advantage of combining these treatments over either approach alone (Davidson et al., 2004).

Table 5
Evidence-Based Pharmacological Treatments for Social Anxiety Disorder

Medication	Initial Daily Dose (and Maximum Daily Dose)	Comments
Citalopram (Celexa)	20 mg (40–60 mg)	• SSRI antidepressant
Escitalopram (Cipralex; Lexapro)	20 mg (40–60 mg)	• SSRI antidepressant
Fluoxetine (Prozac)	20 mg (80 mg)	• SSRI antidepressant • Evidence regarding the use of fluoxetine for SAD is mixed
Fluvoxamine (Luvox)	50 mg (300 mg)	• SSRI antidepressant
Paroxetine (Paxil)	20 mg (60 mg)	• SSRI antidepressant
Sertraline (Zoloft)	50 mg (200 mg)	• SSRI antidepressant
Phenelzine (Nardil)	15 mg (90 mg)	• MAOI antidepressant • Rarely prescribed due to side effects, interactions, and dietary restrictions
Venlafaxine XR (Effexor XR)	37.5–75 mg (225 mg)	• SNRI antidepressant
Clonazepam (Klonapin; Rivotril)	0.25 mg (4 mg)	• Benzodiazepine anxiolytic • May be difficult to discontinue
Alprazolam (Xanax)	0.25 mg (1.5–3.0 mg)	• Benzodiazepine anxiolytic • May be difficult to discontinue
Gabapentin (Neurontin)	900 mg (3600 mg)	• Anticonvulsant

Note: Each medication listed is supported by at least one randomized controlled clinical trial. For each medication, generic names are indicated first, with brand names in parentheses. Initial and maximum recommended dosages are those recommended by Health Canada (see Swinson et al., 2006). SSRI = selective serotonin reuptake inhibitor. MAOI = monoamine oxidase inhibitor, SNRI = serotonin norepinephrine reuptake inhibitor.

3.3 Factors That Influence Treatment Decisions

3.3.1 Age, Sex, and Ethnicity

CBT has been found to be useful for children, adolescents, and adults of all ages. When treating younger children, strategies may need to be adapted to be age-appropriate. CBT appears to be equally effective for males and females with SAD. Little is known about how treatment should be adapted for various racial and ethnic groups. Nevertheless, when working with ethnically diverse clients, it is important for therapists to make an effort to learn about culture-specific presentations that may differ with respect to both verbal communication styles (e.g., the meaning of silence in conversations, volume and tone of voice) and nonverbal communication styles (e.g., smiling, eye contact, personal space). It is also possible that different cultural backgrounds may influence the extent to which a given client responds to a directive treatment such as CBT.

3.3.2   Education

CBT is appropriate for individuals from a wide range of educational backgrounds. For clients with lower levels of education, some strategies may need to be adapted. Specifically, standard thought records and some cognitive strategies may need to be simplified.

3.3.3   Family and Relationship Factors

Generally, people with SAD can be treated effectively without involving family members or significant others. However, it may be useful to include family members in treatment in cases where they are contributing to the individual's anxiety, either by being overly critical of the client or by reinforcing the client's avoidance behavior. For example, if the client's significant other is also socially phobic, he or she may feel threatened as the client begins to improve, and may put subtle pressure on the client not to confront his or her fears. In such cases, addressing these concerns in one or more treatment sessions that include both the client and the significant other may be useful.

3.3.4   Client Preference

It is generally well established that client preferences and expectations for treatment can influence outcome. Therefore, it is useful to take client preferences into account when developing a treatment plan. For example, clients who have a strong preference for one approach over another (e.g., medication versus CBT versus combined treatment; individual treatment versus group treatment) should have their preferences honored where possible after hearing about the advantages and disadvantages of each approach, except in such cases where doing so might be detrimental to the client in some way.

3.3.5   Treatment History

History of previous treatments should be taken into account when making treatment recommendations. If a previous treatment was ineffective, it is important to find out why the treatment didn't work initially (e.g., lack of compliance by the client, poorly administered treatment by the therapist, etc.), so that possible obstacles can be anticipated and dealt with before they occur. If a previous treatment was effective, it is useful to find out from the client which strategies in particular were useful and to build on those in the current therapy.

3.3.6   Ability to Articulate Cognitions

If a client is unable to articulate the thoughts, beliefs, and predictions that contribute to his or her anxiety and fear despite extensive attempts by the therapist to identify these cognitions, the client may still respond to behavioral strategies such as exposure and social skills training. For clients who cannot use the cognitive strategies effectively, behavioral strategies should be emphasized in treatment.

3.3.7   Anxiety Sensitivity and Fear of Sensations

For clients who are anxious about experiencing physical sensations (particularly sensations that might be noticed by others, such as blushing, sweating, and shaking), strategies for targeting fear of sensations should be included in the treatment. These may include cognitive strategies such as challenging beliefs about physical sensations (e.g., "Everyone will notice my blushing") and conducting behavioral experiments to test out the validity of these beliefs, as well as direct exposure to these feared sensations, particularly in social situations. For example, clients who fear shaking in front of others might be encouraged to purposely allow their hands to shake while filling out a form or a check.

3.3.8   Severity of Avoidance and Safety Behaviors

The more severe the client's avoidance and safety behaviors, the more important it is to include exposure as a significant component of the treatment. Exposure should almost always be included as a part of treatment, but the amount of time devoted to exposure-based strategies relative to cognitive strategies should depend on the severity of the client's avoidance. In cases where clients avoid very little despite their anxiety, a greater emphasis on cognitive strategies may be warranted. Similarly, the amount of time and effort spent on eliminating safety behaviors should be related to the extent to which the client depends on these behaviors to manage his or her anxiety.

3.3.9   Social Skills

In most cases, people with SAD respond well to treatment even when formal social skills training is not included as a component of therapy. In fact, social skills may improve on their own as clients practice exposures, work on challenging their anxiety provoking thoughts, and begin to experience a reduction in anxiety. Nevertheless, including formal social skills training, provided in the context of exposure to feared situations, should be included in cases of more severe social skills deficits, and in cases where social skills impairment appears to interfere with the client's ability to benefit from other cognitive and behavioral approaches.

3.3.10 Comorbidity

In cases where a client has multiple problems, it is useful to determine which of these is the predominant problem. The predominant disorder is typically the one that causes the most functional impairment and psychological distress, and the one for which the client wants treatment. In cases where the comorbid problem is more severe than the social anxiety, it is often best to focus on treating the other condition first. On the other hand, treatment of SAD is appropriate when the social anxiety is the primary problem. Though it is possible to work on more than one problem at a time, it is important that the treatment be focused on a manageable number of issues so that progress can be made.

It is also important to assess the degree to which comorbid problems are likely to have an impact on treatment of SAD. For example, if a client's substance use problems make it difficult to attend regular treatment sessions and follow through on homework assignments without self-medicating, it may be important to treat the substance use disorder first, or at least concurrently with the social anxiety. Similarly, if the client is acutely suicidal or has depression that is so severe he or she can barely get out of bed, it is important for the client to achieve some stability in his or her mood before the SAD is tackled. Nevertheless, mild to moderate levels of comorbidity often do not interfere with treatment of SAD, and should not exclude an individual from obtaining such treatment.

3.3.11 Group Versus Individual Treatment

Research supports the use of either group or individual treatment for SAD, and at this point in time, there is not enough data available to say with confidence whether one approach is superior to the other (for a review, see Bieling, McCabe, & Antony, 2006). Factors that should influence the decision of whether to offer group or individual treatment for SAD include availability of group versus individual treatment, the client's willingness to participate in a group, the likelihood of a client being able to participate in a group treatment without compromising the experience for other members of the group (e.g., individuals with significant personality psychopathology might not be a good fit in a SAD group), the extent to which a client appears to be a better fit for individual treatment than group treatment (e.g., perhaps due to comorbid problems, scheduling difficulties, severity of the problem, etc.), and the extent to which having others available during treatment sessions (e.g., for exposure role-plays) is important for a particular client (e.g., having others available during sessions may be less important for clients who have ample opportunities to interact with others during the course of their day-to-day lives).

Group and individual therapies are both effective options for many people with SAD

4

Treatment

This chapter discusses the treatment of SAD, with an emphasis on evidence-based psychological treatments. Treatments that have been investigated for SAD have included primarily cognitive and behavioral interventions. Therefore the focus will be on these particular approaches to treatment. The chapter reviews the specific methods used to treat SAD, with an emphasis on providing practical, step-by-step suggestions for implementing these treatments. In addition, reviews of the research literature on the efficacy of established treatments and predictors of outcome are included. The chapter also discusses pharmacological approaches and treatments involving the combination of cognitive behavioral therapy (CBT) and medication. Finally, this chapter discusses strategies for preventing a return of symptoms after treatment has ended, as well as methods for dealing with potential barriers to successful treatment.

4.1   Methods of CBT

Treatment of SAD typically includes between 10 and 15 weekly sessions, and includes a variety of strategies, such as self-monitoring, psychoeducation, cognitive therapy, exposure-based techniques, and social skills training. This section discusses each of these strategies in detail, as well as relaxation-based approaches, which have been included in a small number of studies. Methods for preventing relapse and recurrence are also reviewed in this section. Table 6 provides a summary of a sample 12-session protocol for treating SAD using CBT in an individual format. This particular outline includes psychoeducation, cognitive restructuring, exposure, and social skills training. Sessions typically last 50 minutes to an hour. Sessions that include in-session exposure practices and role plays may last longer (e.g., 90 minutes to 2 hours). The strategies described in this section have been adapted from protocols by Antony and Swinson (2000), Heimberg and Becker (2002), Hope, Heimberg, and Turk (2006), and others.

Treatment may last longer, particular when social anxiety symptoms are more severe, or when the problem is complicated by comorbidity, life stress, or other issues

4.1.1   Self-Monitoring

CBT requires that clients monitor their thoughts and behaviors to identify appropriate treatment targets, and to measure change over time. The advantage of completing self-monitoring forms or diaries versus simply asking a client to remember his or her experiences from the previous week is that self-monitor-

Table 6
Session-by-Session Summary of Individual CBT for Social Anxiety Disorder

Session	Strategies and Topics Covered
Session 1	• Develop agenda in collaboration with client. • Introduction to SAD treatment (e.g., what to expect from treatment, structure and frequency of sessions, importance of homework). • Psychoeducation – model of SAD, overview of treatment strategies, recommended self-help readings. • Overview of self-monitoring strategies. • Assign new homework – complete monitoring forms, read introductory chapters from self-help readings.
Session 2	• Develop agenda in collaboration with client. • Review of homework. • Psychoeducation – review cognitive model, provide examples of cognitive distortions, and discuss links between client's anxiety and his or her thoughts. • Assign new homework – monitor cognitive distortions, read self-help chapter(s) on cognitive strategies.
Session 3	• Develop agenda in collaboration with client. • Review of homework. • Psychoeducation – review strategies for challenging cognitive distortions. • Assign new homework – practice challenging cognitive distortions on thought records; conduct behavioral experiments to test out particular beliefs.
Session 4	• Develop agenda in collaboration with client. • Review of homework. • Psychoeducation – introduction to exposure. • Develop exposure hierarchy. • In-session exposures and role-plays. • Assign new homework – cognitive restructuring, completion of thought records, conduct behavioral experiments, exposure practices, read self-help chapter(s) on exposure-based strategies.
Session 5 through 9	• Develop agenda in collaboration with client. • Review of homework. • In-session exposures and role-plays. • Assign new homework – cognitive restructuring, completion of thought records, conduct behavioral experiments, exposure practices.
Session 10	• Develop agenda in collaboration with client. • Homework review. • Psychoeducation – introduction to social skills training. • In-session exposures and role-plays, with attention to rehearsing particular social skills. • Develop agenda in collaboration with client.

Table 6 (continued)

	• Homework review. • Psychoeducation – introduction to social skills training. • In-session exposures and role-plays, with attention to rehearsing particular social skills. • Assign new homework – cognitive restructuring, completion of thought records, conduct behavioral experiments, exposure practices with social skills rehearsal, read self-help chapter(s) on social skills training.
Session 11	• Develop agenda in collaboration with client. • Review of homework. • In-session exposures and role-plays, with attention to rehearsing particular social skills. • Homework – cognitive restructuring, completion of thought records, conduct behavioral experiments, and exposure practices with social skills rehearsal.
Session 12	• Develop agenda in collaboration with client. • Review of homework. • Psychoeducation – discuss triggers for relapse and recurrence, review strategies for preventing relapse and recurrence. • Assign new homework – practice relapse prevention strategies.

ing gets around problems related to retrospective recall biases and limitations in memory. People tend to forget the details of their experience over the course of the week, and their memories are often influenced by how they are feeling at the time they are trying to recall a particular event or experience. For example, if clients are feeling particularly anxious on the day of their therapy session, they may be more likely to recall the entire week as having been more difficult, compared to clients who are feeling less anxious on the day of their therapy session. Having clients monitor their experiences in the moment, rather than trying to recall them several days after the event, can circumvent this problem. Other advantages of self-monitoring is that it keeps clients engaged in the treatment process between therapy sessions, it encourages them to notice their symptoms and the variables that affect their symptoms, and it provides them with an opportunity to work through particular treatment strategies and to measure their effectiveness.

> **Self-monitoring helps clients to take notice of variations in anxiety symptoms over the course of the week, and documents improvements**

Examples of monitoring forms are provided in various sections of this chapter (and in the Appendix), where relevant. The format of monitoring can be flexible. For some individuals, it may be difficult to complete standard forms, and recording responses in a less structured diary format may be more useful. For other clients (e.g., children, adults with limited education, clients whose first language is different than the therapist's), monitoring forms may need to be simplified. Some clients may refuse to complete forms altogether, either because they find the process tedious, they are worried about being judged by the therapist for what they record on the forms, or because they find it anxiety provoking to focus on their thoughts, behaviors, and experiences. In these cases, clients should be encouraged to complete at least some self monitoring despite their reluctance. If their reasons for avoiding self-monitoring are anxiety based, then conceptualizing the filling in of forms as an exposure practice may be useful, and completing forms should become easier over time.

4.1.2   Psychoeducation

Psychoeducation involves teaching clients about the nature of anxiety, providing them with a framework with which to understand their own social anxiety, helping them to understand the relationships among their anxiety symptoms, anxiety provoking thoughts, and anxiety-reducing behaviors, and teaching them about effective strategies for dealing with their anxiety. Self-help books (e.g., Antony, 2004; Antony & Swinson, 2008) can also be used to reinforce material discussed during treatment sessions.

Presenting the Treatment Rationale
An important focus of the first treatment session in CBT is the presentation of the treatment rationale. Key points to be covered during the first session include the following:

- Anxiety is normal, and everyone experiences anxiety from time to time, in various situations. It is also normal to feel anxious in social situations, and most people report feeling shy, nervous, or anxious at times about the possibility of being judged by others (Zimbardo, Pilkonis, & Norwood, 1975). Most people also report experiencing physical symptoms of anxiety in social situations (Purdon, Antony, Monteiro, & Swinson, 2001). Social anxiety is characterized by attempts to control anxiety or prevent anxiety from occurring. Successful treatment often involves becoming more accepting of one's anxiety, rather than trying to control it.

Clients should be encouraged to think of their anxiety as being normal, and even helpful in certain situations

- Rather than thinking about anxiety as something to be avoided, it is useful to recognize that anxiety actually helps us to survive in the world. All of the symptoms that are experienced when one is anxious or frightened help the individual or organism to survive in the face of possible danger or social threat, by preparing the body for escape or for meeting the threat head on, perhaps with an aggressive response (this is often referred to as the "fight or flight" response). When we are anxious, our hearts race to get blood to larger muscles. We begin to breathe more quickly in order to increase oxygen levels to meet the demands of the situation. We sweat to cool off the body so we can physically perform more efficiently. In addition to these general benefits of anxiety, social anxiety in particular also has advantages. Apprehension about making a bad impression on others helps us to avoid saying things or doing things that might lead to being negatively evaluated or even being ostracized from a group. Anxiety also motivates us to prepare for a social challenge (e.g., a job interview) and to perform the best we possibly can. Social anxiety is only a problem when it occurs so frequently and so intensely that it interferes with an individual's life, such that the costs of the anxiety outweigh the benefits. Therefore, the goal of treatment is not to eliminate all anxiety, but rather to bring anxiety down to a level where it no longer causes significant impairment.

- Anxiety consists of three components: the *physical* component (what we feel), the *cognitive* component (what we think), and the *behavioral* component (what we do).
- The *physical component* of anxiety includes all of the physical sensations that people experience when they are nervous or frightened, including a racing heart, shortness of breath, dizziness, blushing, shaking, and sweating, for example. These symptoms are perfectly normal and completely safe. They occur during anxiety, but they also occur in the context of other intense emotions (e.g., anger), during sexual arousal, during exercise, as well as in other situations.
- The *cognitive component* of anxiety refers to the thoughts, assumptions, beliefs, and predictions than an individual holds about the situations he or she fears or about his or her performance (e.g., "it is important that everybody likes me," "it would be terrible to make a mistake during my presentation"), as well as about the symptoms of anxiety themselves (e.g., "I need to control my shaking," "people will think I'm disgusting if I sweat at the party"). The cognitive component also includes any biases in attention or memory that influence a person's anxiety. People tend to pay more attention to information that confirms their beliefs and to remember such information as compared to information that is inconsistent with their beliefs. They may also purposely seek out information that confirms their beliefs. For example, during a presentation a socially anxious client may scan the audience for individuals who appear to be bored or to disapprove of their presentation.
- The *behavioral component* of anxiety refers to behaviors that individuals use to prevent their anxiety from occurring, to reduce the intensity of anxiety after it has begun, or to prevent other negative consequences from occurring. These behaviors may include avoidance, escape, or overreliance on safety behaviors (e.g., overpreparing for a presentation, wearing excessive amounts of makeup to hide blushing, etc.).
- The physical, cognitive, and behavioral components interact with one another, and the cycle of anxiety can begin with any one of the three components. For example, a sensation of sweating may trigger beliefs about being noticed and negatively evaluated by others, which in turn may trigger an escape from the situation. Similarly, a thought that others will negatively evaluate one's presentation may lead to physical sensations such as shaking and blushing, which in turn can lead to increased anxiety and an avoidance response. Clients can use the Three Components of Anxiety Monitoring Form to monitor these experiences (see Appendix).
- From a cognitive behavioral perspective, anxiety is not triggered by situations and events alone, but rather by our interpretations and beliefs about these events. In particular, anxiety occurs when a situation is perceived as dangerous or threatening. Sometimes these perceptions are accurate, and other times they are not. In the case of excessive social anxiety, individuals believe that it is very important to make a good impression

At the start of treatment, it is important to present clients with a model that provides a CBT framework for understanding their social anxiety

on others, that they are likely to behave in a way that is embarrassing and humiliating, and that the consequences of their behavior will be disastrous (Clark & Wells, 1995). They make negative predictions about what might happen in social situations, they tend to be overly focused on themselves when in social situations, and they dwell on everything that might have gone wrong after a social interaction has ended. In addition, anxious behaviors (e.g., avoidance, escape, safety behaviors) serve to keep the social anxiety alive by preventing individuals from ever learning that feared situations are actually much safer than they seem, feared consequences are unlikely to come true, and that the individual probably can cope with such consequences if they do occur.

- Effective treatment strategies are designed to directly target the three components of anxiety and fear. Cognitive strategies help people to replace their anxiety provoking thoughts and predictions with more realistic beliefs. Once beliefs about social situations begin to change, anxiety levels will decrease. Exposure-based strategies require people to reduce their avoidance behaviors by directly confronting the situations and sensations they fear. In doing so, individuals discover that their feared consequences do not come true, which leads to changes in their anxiety-provoking thoughts, and ultimately in their overall levels of anxiety. Social skills training provides people with an opportunity to improve their performance in social situations, thereby reducing the likelihood of feared consequences occurring, and increasing the individual's confidence. Finally, strategies such as medication use and relaxation training directly impact upon the physical component of anxiety, perhaps by reducing symptoms of arousal.

4.1.3   Cognitive Strategies

Although there are a number of cognitive psychotherapies, the strategies described in this section are most closely related to those developed by Aaron T. Beck and colleagues (e.g., Beck, Emery, & Greenberg, 1985). The primary goal of cognitive therapy is to teach clients to identify their anxious thoughts, to consider the evidence regarding these thoughts, and to replace unrealistic or exaggerated beliefs about possible danger with more realistic thoughts, beliefs, and predictions. Clients are encouraged to think of their beliefs as hypotheses, rather than facts, and to consider a range of possible interpretations and outcomes instead of automatically assuming that the worst is likely to happen.

Instead of simply telling clients what they "should" be thinking, cognitive therapy involves the use of Socratic questioning to help clients arrive at their own conclusions based on the evidence. Examples of Socratic questions that can be used to help clients to challenge their anxious thoughts include:

- Are there other ways of thinking about that situation?
- How might someone without social anxiety think about this situation?
- Are your thoughts consistent with the evidence or with previous experiences?
- What else might occur, other than your feared outcome?

- What does your past experience tell you about the likelihood of _____ occurring?
- What might you say to a friend who was nervous about having shaky hands at a party? Would you recommend that she never go to another party?
- What if you were to sweat during your presentation? Realistically, would it be as awful as you imagine? Would it still matter the next day? The next week? The next month? Would there be any terrible consequences?
- What if someone noticed you making a mistake? For how long would the person think about you? Would your mistake be the most important thing that's happened in that person's day? What other things might that person be concerned about?
- What if your job interview goes poorly and you don't get the job? How could you cope with that? Does the possibility of that happening mean that you should never apply for a job?
- What if _____ actually finds you boring? Why would that be a problem? What would it mean about you? Are there are other ways of thinking about that?
- Can you think of advantages of staying at the party despite your anxiety?

Table 7 describes a variety of cognitive strategies that can be used to challenge anxiety provoking thoughts and predictions in people with SAD. In addition, the Appendix includes an illustration of the steps in examining the evidence for anxious thoughts.

Table 7
Examples of Cognitive Strategies for Social Anxiety Disorder

Strategy	Description
Cognitive Restructuring	- Involves asking Socratic questions designed to help the client to recognize that (a) feared outcomes may be unlikely to occur, and (b) he or she would be able to cope with many of his or her feared outcomes if they actually were to occur. - Also involves completion of thought records on which clients record their anxiety-provoking thoughts, alternative thoughts, and the evidence for and against both the anxious thoughts and the alternative thoughts. The goal of using the thought records is to reduce anxiety by learning to think about feared situations in less anxious ways.
Behavioral Experiment	- Involves designing and executing experiments to test out whether a particular thought is true. - Example – doing something to draw attention to oneself (e.g., spilling a glass of water, dropping keys, yelling to someone across a crowded room) to assess whether the belief "it would be terrible to do anything to draw attention to myself" is in fact true.

Table 7 (continued)	
Perspective Shifting	• Involves asking a client to take the perspective of someone who is not anxious and to think about the situations that make him or her anxious from the alternative perspective. • Examples: (a) ask the client how his or her friend (who is not anxious in social situations) might think about a particular anxiety provoking situation, (b) ask the client what he or she might say to someone else who reported a thought or prediction similar to that of the client, (c) ask the client to participate in a role play simulation in which he or she plays the role of the therapist and the therapist plays the role of the client.
Coping Statements	• Involves having the client record realistic statements (perhaps derived through earlier cognitive restructuring) that can be used as quick reminders when feeling anxious. • Examples of coping statements might include: (a) it is okay if not everyone likes me, (b) it is normal to sweat, shake, or blush in front of others from time to time, (c) I don't have to be perfect.

Thought Records

Figure 2 provides an example of a social anxiety thought record that can be used to help people with SAD challenge their anxiety provoking thoughts whenever they feel anxious about a social situation (a blank copy is reprinted in the Appendix). In the first column, the client records the date and time when the situation arose, and in the second column the client provides a brief description of the situation. In the third column, any anxiety provoking thoughts and predictions are recorded, followed in column four by a rating of how anxious the client was (on a scale from 0 to 100). In the next three columns, the client records alternative (nonanxious) beliefs and predictions, evidence and rational conclusions regarding this situation, and his or her anxiety level after going through the exercise of challenging anxious thinking (again, using a scale ranging from 0 to 100).

Although treatment of SAD includes a number of different strategies, the therapist should take advantage of opportunities to challenge anxious thinking whenever possible. For example, during the homework review at the start of each session, anxious thinking should be challenged. Similarly, clients should be encouraged to challenge their anxiety-provoking predictions during exposure practices.

Core Beliefs

Core beliefs are deeply held assumptions that affect how an individual interprets most situations that he or she encounters

In addition to challenging anxious thinking related to particular social situations, clients often have more deeply held beliefs that color how they see themselves and many of the situations that arise in their day-to-day lives. These beliefs are often referred to as *core beliefs* or *schemas*. Examples of core beliefs that are often seen in people with SAD include beliefs such as:

Day and Time	Situation	Anxiety-Provoking Thoughts and Predictions	Anxiety Before (0–00)	Alternative Thoughts and Predictions	Evidence and Realistic Conclusions	Anxiety After (0–100)
July 12 9 pm	I am sweaty at a party.	• People will notice I'm sweaty. • If they notice me sweating, they'll think I'm anxious and weak. • It would be terrible to have others think that I am anxious and weak. • I need to leave this situation before someone notices my sweating.	90	• People may not even notice that I'm sweating. • If they do notice, they may think I am hot or that I am not feeling well. • Even if some people think I am anxious and weak, it wouldn't be the end of the world. • I can stay in this situation despite my anxiety.	• Nobody has mentioned that they notice my sweating, not even my wife. • I notice a couple of other people who seem a bit hot or sweaty. I also notice that some people at the party seem less comfortable than others. • People sweat for all sorts of reasons. I don't think other people are anxious and weak just because they are sweating. • It is impossible for everyone to think positively about me all the time. It is okay if some people think I am anxious or weak. • If I stay in the situation, chances are that my anxiety will decrease. It usually does.	50

Figure 2
Social Anxiety Thought Record. © 2007 Martin M. Antony. Reprinted with permission.

- I am incompetent.
- I am boring.
- I am unlovable.
- People are generally mean, and they think the worst about others.
- People expect me to be perfect.

Although clients may spontaneously reveal their core beliefs, more often than not, core beliefs need to be uncovered or inferred. One strategy for uncovering core beliefs involves looking for themes across the negative automatic thoughts that a client reports about various situations. For example, if a client repeatedly describes fears of others finding him or her boring, it may be an indication that the client believes that he or she is boring. Another strategy that can be used to reveal negative core beliefs is the *downward arrow technique*, in which the client is repeatedly asked questions about the meaning of his or her negative automatic thoughts. The following interaction illustrates this process.

Clinical Vignette
Downward Arrow Technique

Client: I am very worried about my presentation.
Therapist: What are you afraid will happen?
Client: I will lose my train of thought.
Therapist: Why would that be a problem?
Client: People will think I am anxious.
Therapist: Why would that matter?
Client: If they see me as anxious, they will think I am weak.
Therapist: What would that mean about you?
Client: It would mean that I *am* weak.

Shifting core beliefs can be more difficult than challenging the negative automatic thoughts that arise in particular situations, but the strategies for doing so are somewhat similar (e.g., Greenberger & Padesky, 1995). Techniques for challenging core beliefs include (a) encouraging the client to keep a positive data log in which he or she records evidence throughout the day that demonstrates that the negative core belief is not 100% true, (b) encouraging the client to identify and strengthen alternative core beliefs (e.g., I am competent) by recording evidence that supports the alternative core belief, (c) reviewing evidence for the negative and alternative core beliefs across the client's life, and (d) conducting behavioral experiments to test out the validity of the negative and alternative core beliefs (this new evidence can be added to the positive data log).

Troubleshooting

Cognitive strategies are usually quite effective for helping clients shift their anxious thinking. However, certain challenges and obstacles may arise when using cognitive therapy. Table 8 provides examples of obstacles that may interfere with the cognitive strategies and some suggestions for dealing with these issues.

Table 8
Cognitive Therapy Obstacles and Possible Solutions

Obstacle	Possible Solutions and Considerations
Client cannot identify specific thoughts	• Ask questions to identify thoughts (e.g., What do you think might happen if you were to go to a party? What might others think of you?). • Probe for anxiety-provoking imagery (e.g., What images go through you mind? Can you imagine a scene in which you arrive late for class? What do you see happening?). • Suggest that the client try a behavioral challenge, a role play simulation, or an exposure practice, and ask about the client's thoughts when the anxiety is activated. • Suggest possible thoughts and assess their relevance (e.g., other people with social anxiety sometimes worry that others will think they are stupid, boring, incompetent, weak, or unattractive in some other way. Do you worry about any of these?).
Cognitive restructuring does not lead to anxiety reduction	• Assess whether the thoughts being targeted during cognitive restructuring are the most relevant thoughts (also known as the "hot thoughts"). • Assess whether the client is discounting the alternative thoughts generated through cognitive restructuring (e.g., yes, but...) • Assess whether there is additional information or evidence that could be brought into the cognitive restructuring process. • Consider relying more heavily on behavioral strategies, such as exposure.
Client does not complete thought records	• Assess reasons for noncompliance. • If noncompliance is due to anxiety caused by completing the forms, encourage the client to complete the forms despite the anxiety. The process should become easier over time (see the next section on exposure-based strategies). • If noncompliance is due to competing demands, use problem solving to improve compliance (e.g., schedule a consistent time each day to complete the forms). • If the thought record is too intellectually challenging for a client, consider simplifying the form, or using a different method of recording (e.g., recording experiences in writing using a diary or verbally using a tape recorder). • If the client is not completing the forms, but is using the strategies effectively in his or her day-to-day life, the lack of compliance with the completion of thought records may not be a problem.
Client is too anxious to use cognitive restructuring in social situations	• Practice cognitive restructuring before entering the situation, or after the situation has ended. • Rely on simpler strategies (e.g., coping statements) when in the situation. • Try to practice the cognitive strategies in less anxiety-provoking situations.

Table 8 (continued)	
Client avoids situations and therefore anxiety is not being activated	• Suggest that the client practice exposure to activate anxiety and anxiety provoking thoughts, thereby providing an opportunity to practice challenging the thoughts. • Use examples of previous anxiety-provoking scenarios that were not avoided to practice using cognitive restructuring.

4.1.4　Exposure-Based Strategies

Repeated exposure to feared situations usually leads to a reduction in fear and anxiety

Perhaps the most powerful method of reducing fear is by directly confronting the situations, thoughts, and sensations that an individual fears and avoids. Although there are a number of explanations for how exposure works (see Moscovitch, Antony, & Swinson, in press), from a cognitive behavioral perspective exposure is believed to reduce fear and anxiety by providing a corrective experience that contradicts a client's anxiety-provoking thoughts and predictions. Essentially, the client learns that his or her feared consequences rarely occur (e.g., the client doesn't make a fool of himself), and even when bad things happen (e.g., people make a mistake and get laughed at), the situation is more manageable than the client had expected.

Generating Exposure Practices

One of the challenges in using exposure therapy is the generation of appropriate exposure practices. Table 9 includes examples of exposure practices that target fear in particular types of social situations.

Table 9
Examples of Exposure Practices for Social Anxiety Disorder

Feared Situation	Examples of Exposure Practices
Public speaking	• Attend Toastmasters meetings (see www.toastmaster.org). • Take a public speaking course or drama class. • Offer to give a lecture at a high school or elementary school about one's work. • Speak up in meetings at work (e.g., ask questions or volunteer to present some relevant material). • Give a toast at a dinner party. • Ask questions in class. • Read in front of a group.
Small talk and casual conversation	• Arrive at work early and chat with coworkers. • Take advantage of opportunities to attend parties, outings, and get-togethers with friends, coworkers, and acquaintances. • Talk to strangers in public places, such as elevators, lines, and other places. For example, ask what time it is, ask for directions, compliment the other person, or talk about the weather.

Table 9 (continued)

	• Practice joining other conversations that are ongoing (e.g., at a party or gathering). • Attend a gallery opening, a public meeting, or some other gathering of strangers.
Being observed in public	• Walk down a busy street. • Cross the street at a busy intersection. • Shop in a busy mall or supermarket. • Work out in a crowded gym. • Attend a concern or sporting event. • Sit in a park or coffee shop.
Being the center of attention	• Make a mistake in public (e.g., spill a glass of water, drop keys, purposely lose train of thought, knock something over). • Play a party game (e.g., Pictionary, Outburst, charades). • Call out to another person from across a crowded room. • Arrive late to a meeting. • Wear clothing that is likely to attract comments (e.g., bright colors, mismatched clothes, incorrectly buttoned shirts).
Dating and meeting new people	• Talk to others who might be possible targets for friendship or dating. • Join an online dating service, answer personal ads. • Join a club or take a class where you might meet people with similar interests (e.g., a fitness club, hockey team, book club, photography class, etc.). • Ask a coworker or acquaintance out for lunch, a coffee, drink, or movie. • Offer to drive an acquaintance home from a party or from work.
Eating or drinking in front of others	• Go out for lunch, dinner, or drinks with friends or colleagues. • Eat in a crowded restaurant or food court. • Eat messy foods in front of others. • Purposely allow hands to shake while holding a drink. • Eat or drink in front of others at work or school.
Writing in front of others	• Fill out a check in front of others. • Fill out a form (e.g., a credit card application, a contest ballot) in front of others. • Write a letter while sitting in a public place (e.g., a coffee shop). • Sign documents in front of colleagues. • Purposely allow hands to shake while writing in front of others.
Potential conflict situations	• Drive slowly on a busy street (but be careful not to endanger yourself or other drivers). • Do multiple transactions at a bank machine when the line is long. • Return an item to a store. • Take a long time to make a decision when ordering dinner in a restaurant. • Have a cashier ring up some items in a store and then explain that you have left your wallet at home.

Exposure Hierarchies

An important tool in exposure therapy is the *exposure hierarchy*. An exposure hierarchy is a list of situations that an individual fears and avoids, rank ordered from situations that produce mild anxiety at the bottom of the list, to situations that produce extreme anxiety at the top of the list. For each item, clients provide a fear rating (e.g., using a scale ranging from 0–100), and the order of items is determined by these ratings. Some hierarchies include separate ratings for fear and avoidance. However for most individuals fear and avoidance are highly correlated, and there is little benefit of including separate ratings for these dimensions. Typically, exposure hierarchies include 10 to 15 items. Items should generally reflect situations in which the client would like to feel more comfortable, and that are practical and easy to arrange during the course of treatment. For example, "getting married" would not be an appropriate hierarchy item for client who is not currently in a relationship. Items on the hierarchy should also be as specific as possible. For example, "going to a party with my wife at the home of a coworker, without drinking any alcohol" would be a more useful item than "going to a party." Table 10 presents an example of an exposure hierarchy for SAD. A blank Exposure Hierarchy Form is provided in the Appendix.

Hierarchies are often used to guide exposure practices. Clients begin exposures with items in the bottom half of their hierarchy, and as situations become easier, they progress to more difficult situations. It is not necessary to start with items right at the bottom of the hierarchy. In fact, clients can start as high as they are willing to. It is also not necessary to practice items in order. Items can also be added and deleted as the client progresses through treatment and it becomes apparent that changes to the hierarchy are warranted. The hierarchy

Table 10
Example of an Exposure Hierarchy for Social Anxiety Disorder

Number	Item Description	Fear Rating (0–100)
1	Go out on a blind date.	100
2	Invite four or five people from work to my home.	90
3	See a movie with Parker.	85
4	Have lunch with four or five coworkers.	85
5	Have lunch with Cindy.	80
6	Express an opinion during the weekly staff meeting.	70
7	Discuss my weekend with coworkers on Monday morning.	65
8	Ask strangers for directions at the mall.	50
9	Make comments to strangers about the weather on an elevator.	50
10	Walk down a busy street alone with my hat on backwards.	40

can also be used as a measure of change by having the client rerate the items at each session, or less often (e.g., every third or fourth session).

Guidelines for Effective Exposure

Not all exposure is helpful. In fact, exposure can lead to an increase in fear or anxiety depending on the way it is done. For example, being rejected after spending months working up the courage to ask somebody out on a date can be devastating for somebody with SAD. To get the most out of exposure it is important for clients to follow a few key guidelines. Research evidence concerning these guidelines is reviewed in more detail elsewhere (e.g., Antony & Swinson, 2000; Moscovitch et al., in press). A client handout summarizing these and other guidelines is provided in the Appendix. An Exposure Monitoring Form is also provided in the Appendix.

Frequency of exposure practices. Exposure seems to work best when sessions are scheduled close together. For example, in a study of individuals with agoraphobia, it was found that 10 daily exposure practices were significantly more effective than 10 weekly exposure practices, even though clients received the same amount of exposure in both conditions (Foa, Jameson, Turner, & Payne, 1980). Generally we recommended that clients engage in major exposure practices (e.g., eating out with colleagues) at least three to four times per week, and small exposure practices (e.g., saying hello to strangers on the elevator) whenever opportunities arise. If exposures are too infrequent, return of fear between practices will be significant, and each practice will seem like starting over. However, if exposures are frequent, they tend to build on one another, and each practice tends to be easier than the one before.

Length of exposure practices. Longer exposures tend to work better than shorter exposures. Generally, exposures should last long enough to learn that one's feared consequences do not come true, or to learn that it is possible to cope in a situation despite high levels of anxiety. Often, an individual's anxiety will decrease over the course of an exposure practice. However, recent evidence suggests that it is not necessary to experience a reduction in fear and anxiety during any particular practice in order to experience improvement across practices (Craske & Mystkowski, 2006). The length of an exposure practice generally depends on the type of situation. For example, a client who is working on decreasing anxiety at parties may choose to stay at a party for several hours, perhaps arriving at the beginning of a party and staying at least until people start to leave. On the other hand, an individual who is afraid of asking for directions might stand in a mall or some other public place and practice asking people for directions repeatedly, for 30 to 60 minutes. The key is to stay until the anxiety is decreased, or until the individual has learned that the situation is manageable. Generally, the longer an exposure lasts, the more beneficial it is.

Perceived control and predictability. As reviewed by Antony and Swinson (2000), there is evidence that fear reduction during exposure practices is related to a client's perception of control in a situation, as well as the extent to which events seem predictable during the practice. Perceived control can be enhanced by helping clients to recognize that they are more socially skilled than they assume, and they do have some control over what happens to them in social situations. Cognitive strategies can be useful in this regard. People with SAD also have control over the duration of their exposures, since they can leave at any time (of course, the therapist should encourage clients to stay in the situation). Though it is difficult for clients to be able to predict with certainty how others will respond to them in social situations, they can make an effort to imagine various outcomes and how they might cope with them, before entering a feared situation. For example, before asking someone else out on a date, the client should be encouraged to imagine all of the possible ways that the other person might respond, and how he or she might cope with each of these responses. Being prepared for a wide range of responses will help the client to deal with possible rejection.

Eliminating safety behaviors. In the context of CBT, safety behaviors are thought to have the same function as avoidance. Specifically, they help to maintain the belief that social situations are dangerous by preventing individuals from ever learning what might happen in these situations if they were not to engage in their safety behaviors. In SAD, reducing safety behaviors during exposure practices lead to greater improvements in anxiety and reductions in the perception of social threat (Garcia-Palacios & Botella, 2003; Morgan & Raffle, 1999; Wells et al., 1995). Therefore clients should be encouraged to begin to let go of their safety behaviors (e.g., alcohol use to manage anxiety, covering up blushing, etc.). This process can occur gradually, and can be built into the hierarchy. For example, in early exposures people may continue to use their safety behaviors, and only eliminate those behaviors as they start to become more comfortable.

Focus on the task rather than the outcome. Although one goal of CBT is for clients to learn that the outcomes they fear are unlikely, another goal is to learn that these outcomes do occur from time to time, and that they are often more manageable than previously assumed. Clients should be encouraged to recognize that completing more exposure practices will likely lead to more frequent rejections (after all, complete avoidance is associated with a complete lack of rejection). The initial goal of exposure practices should not be to get a date, land a job, or win over an audience. Of course, as the individual becomes more comfortable and his or her skills improve, the individual will start to enjoy more positive consequences as well. Following successful treatment, clients will be more willing to risk the possibility of rejection, and will be better able to cope when they are evaluated negatively by others. Clients should think of a successful exposure is one in which they confront a feared situation despite their anxiety, regardless of the outcome. They should expect to feel uncomfortable, and should resist the temptation to fight their anxiety or to try to "make" it go away.

> **Exposure is most effective when practices are predictable, prolonged, and frequent, and when safety behaviors are eliminated**

Simulated Exposures (Role Plays)

In addition to exposures conducted in actual feared situations, simulated exposures or role plays are often used in the treatment of SAD. In simulated exposures, it is necessary to identify others to participate. These may include the therapist, friends, colleagues, family members, colleagues of the therapist, or other clients (in the case of group therapy). Exposure role-plays give clients an opportunity to practice exposure in a less threatening context, before trying it in a real situation where the risk is greater. Exposure simulations also give clients an opportunity to practice particular social skills or tasks (e.g., asking someone out on a date, telling a joke) in relative safety, with nothing to lose. An advantage of simulated exposures is the ability to control the difficulty of the practice. For example, when practicing simulated job interviews, it is possible to vary the difficulty of the practice by having the interviewer be either supportive or aggressive. In addition to simulated job interviews, other examples of role play exposures include practicing a presentation in front of one's family, making small talk with the therapist acting as a stranger, or role playing a phone call to one's insurance company with a friend playing the role of the insurance staff person.

Symptom Exposure

Exposure to feared symptoms (also called *interoceptive exposure*) has been found to improve anxiety about physical sensations among people with panic disorder (see Antony & Swinson, 2000). Although there has been little research on the effects of symptom exposure for people with SAD, symptom exposure is often used clinically for individuals who are frightened of experiencing particular sensations in social situations. For example, people who are afraid of sweating in front of others might be encouraged to wear warm clothing in social situations to learn that it is okay to sweat in front of other people. They might even wet their foreheads or underarms before going into social situations to learn that nothing bad actually happens when one appears sweaty. People who are frightened of blushing in front of others might do things to make their faces red, such as eating spicy foods, eating hot soup, wearing blush, holding their breath, or exercising. People who fear shaking in front of others might be encouraged to purposely shake their hands as they speak in front of a group, hold a drink, fill out a form, or sign their names. Specific exercises have been developed for inducing a wide range of sensations that people often experience when feeling anxious (see Antony, Ledley, Liss, & Swinson, 2006). Generally, people with SAD are not frightened of physical sensations when they are not in the company of others. Therefore, when treating SAD, symptom exposure should be combined with situational exposure practices.

Exposure to feared sensations, such as sweating, may be useful for people who fear these symptoms, especially when combined with situational exposure

Troubleshooting

A number of issues can interfere with a client's progress during exposure therapy. Table 11 provides a list of possible obstacles, along with strategies for overcoming these challenges.

Table 11
Exposure Therapy Obstacles and Possible Solutions

Obstacle	Possible Solutions
Fear doesn't decrease during an exposure practice	• Increase the length of the practice. • Assess whether the client is relying on safety behaviors during the practice, and if so attempt to eliminate these behaviors. • Assess the degree to which a client's anxious thoughts and predictions are contributing to the lack of fear reduction, and address these using cognitive strategies.

Table 11 (continued)

	• Note that fear reduction during a particular exposure practice is not necessary for long-term benefit from exposure therapy. If fear does not decrease despite attempting some of the solutions already discussed, resume exposure practices at the next session.
Fear returns between exposure practices	• It is normal for some degree of fear to return between exposure practices. If return of fear is significant, assess whether life is events or circumstances (e.g., a critical boss, an abusive partner) are contributing to the return of fear. Also, consider scheduling exposure practices more frequently.
Client refuses to do a particular practice	• Negotiate with the client to come up with a new practice, that is challenging but manageable. • Ask the client whether the proposed practice can be altered in some way to make it more manageable.
Client requests to end the practice due to fear	• Encourage the client to continue the practice by providing reassurance that his or her fear will decrease over time. • Use cognitive strategies to bring the fear down to a manageable level. • Alter aspects of the situation to bring the fear down to a manageable level. • If the client ends up terminating the exposure practice, encourage him or her to enter the situation again as soon as possible.
Client is not fearful of the practice	• Exposure requires fear activation to be effective. If a client is not fearful of a particular practice, alter aspects of the situation to make the practice more challenging, or attempt a different practice from the client's hierarchy.
The situation is too brief for prolonged exposure	• Exposure practices are most effective when they are prolonged. In the case of a brief exposure (e.g., asking for directions, paying for items in a store, standing in line), it is best to repeat the practice over and over, until the client's anxiety has decreased or the client has learned that his or her fear consequences do not occur.
Social skills impairments interfere with exposure outcomes	• Clients with significant social skills impairment may find that their feared consequences do occur on a regular basis (e.g., a client who avoids all eye contact may find that others show no interest in talking to him or her). In these cases, it may be important to work on social skills impairments during exposure practices (e.g., encouraging the client to make more eye contact when talking to others).

4.1.5   Social Skills Training

Social skills training is based on the assumption that social anxiety is, in part, related to impairments in social skills, which in turn lead to negative reactions from others, thereby confirming the individual's view of him or herself as inadequate. Social skills training involves identifying behaviors to target, educating clients about appropriate social behavior, encouraging clients to practice new social behaviors, and providing feedback to the client about his or her use of these strategies. Social skills are typically rehearsed in the context of simulated role play exposures as well as real life exposure practices. Often, practices are videotaped so clients can view their own performance. Videotaping is useful because it provides clients with an opportunity to more objectively judge the quality of their performance, relative to making such judgments without actual data. Videotaping also provides the therapist with opportunities to provide clients visual examples of behaviors that need to be worked on. Examples of social skills that are often targeted during social skills training are provided in Table 12. A number of excellent self-help guides are available for improving social and communication skills (e.g., McKay, Davis, & Fanning, 1995).

A number of established protocols for treating SAD have included social skills training as a component (e.g., Turner, Beidel, Cooley-Quille, Woody, & Messer, 1994), though some others have not (e.g., Heimberg et al., 1990). Meta-analytic studies (e.g., Taylor, 1996) have generally found no advantage of social skill training over other CBT strategies, though a recent study found that CBT with social skills training as a component was more effective than CBT without social skill training (Herbert et al., 2005).

Table 12
Examples of Social Skills Targeted in Social Skills Training

Social Skill	Examples of Behavioral Goals
Nonverbal communication	• Improving frequency of eye contact. • Learning to lean forward when sitting with others. • Standing closer to others. • Smiling more frequently (or less frequently in clients with a tendency to smile or laugh when nervous). • Sitting up straight.
Speech patterns	• Learning to speak with a confident tone. • Increasing the volume of speech (for clients who speak too quietly). • Speaking with more expressiveness in one's tone.
Conversation skills	• Using conversation starters – strategies for breaking the ice. • Being able to generate ideas for small talk. • Learning strategies for ending conversations gracefully. • Apologizing less frequently (for clients who tend to tend to apologize constantly – even when they haven't done anything that requires an apology).

Table 12 (continued)

Listening skills	• Maintaining eye contact when listening to others. • Conveying understanding and empathy when listing to others. • Avoiding barriers to effective listening, including comparing oneself to the other individual, rehearsing what to say next, changing the subject, filtering what the other person says, etc.
Assertiveness skills	• Stating one's needs without being perceived as pushy or aggressive. • Using the "broken record" technique – repeat one's needs without excessively justifying or explaining one's perspective. • Confronting issues directly with other people, rather than passively. • Learning to listen assertively, with a commitment to understand the other person's perspective. • Learning to validate the other person's feelings.
Conflict skills	• Choosing appropriate times to discuss sensitive issues. • Staying focused on the problem at hand. • Using cognitive strategies to examine whether one's perspective is realistic. • Deciding whether a confrontation is worth the potential consequences. • Trying to understand the other individual's perspective. • Bouncing ideas off a neutral third party before discussing the issue with the other individual.
Interview skills	• Preparing for job interviews (e.g., learning about the employer, preparing a list of questions, identifying one's strengths). • Listening to what the interviewer asks and says. • Dressing appropriately for the interview. • Knowing how to answer personal questions. • Learning to appear confident, flexible, courteous, and tactful. • Managing the postinterview phase appropriately (e.g., following up with the interviewer).
Dating skills	• Developing strategies for meeting new people (e.g., networking, personal ads, joining clubs or taking classes). • Improving conversation skills. • Managing issues that arise during different stages of dating (e.g., the first meeting versus knowing the person for several months). • Dealing with rejection.
Presentation skills	• Preparing for the presentation (e.g., understanding the purpose of the presentation, understanding the audience, preparing slides or other materials, rehearsing, using CBT strategies to manage anxiety). • Make sure that all words are pronounced correctly, that voice volume doesn't drop off, that rate of speech is appropriate, and that words such as "um" and "uh" are avoided.

Table 12 (continued)

- Increasing expressiveness in one's tone.
- Making eye contact with audience members.
- Walking around during the presentation, and gesturing with one's hands.
- Resisting the temptation to read the presentation verbatim.
- Repeating the main points frequently.
- Resisting the temptation to fit in too much information.
- Avoiding the tendency to talk down to the audience, while being sure to explain new concepts fully.
- Being prepared to answer questions.
- Being genuine (i.e., not trying *too* hard to be entertaining).
- Using humor where appropriate.

4.1.6   Relaxation and Arousal Management Strategies

Generally, there is much less research on relaxation-based strategies for SAD than there is for the other strategies reviewed thus far. Nevertheless, there are a few studies suggesting that applied muscle relaxation may be useful for this problem (Jerremalm, Johansson, & Öst, 1980; Osberg, 1981). Applied relaxation involves combining relaxation strategies with graduated exposure to increasingly challenging situations. Because applied relaxation includes practices in stressful situations, it is not clear whether the benefits of applied relaxation in SAD are due to the relaxation strategies or the repeated exposure to feared situations. There are no studies investigating whether relaxation training adds any benefit over and above the effects of exposure alone. However, in other anxiety disorders, research comparing exposure with relaxation training versus exposure alone have tended to find little benefit of adding relaxation training to exposure (for a review, see Antony & Swinson, 2000).

> **Little is known about whether relaxation-based strategies are useful in the treatment of SAD**

Although the addition of relaxation training in the treatment of phobic disorders is not well supported, progressive muscle relaxation, breathing retraining, and similar strategies for reducing arousal have been found to be effective as general strategies for managing stress and anxiety in GAD (Rowa & Antony, in press). Progressive muscle relaxation involves teaching a client to alternately tense and relax a series of muscle groups (e.g., arms, legs, torso, neck, shoulders, face, etc.). During each tension-relaxation pairing, the individual is instructed to focus on the particular muscle group and on the sensations he or she is experiencing. During the relaxation phase of each pairing, the individual focuses on becoming more and more relaxed, and on allowing the feelings of relaxation to spread throughout the body. After completing the series of tension-relaxation exercises, a number of additional exercises involving breathing and meditation are used to further facilitate reaching a state of complete relaxation. As the individual becomes proficient at using a series of exercises to relax, the exercises are made briefer by focusing on a smaller number of muscle groups, then on eliminating the tension component of the exercises, and then on eliminating the sequential focus on particular muscle groups. By the end of treatment, the individual is able to relax with a single breath. A detailed description of progressive muscle relaxation is available elsewhere (Bernstein, Borkovec, & Hazlett-Stevens, 2000).

A second relaxation method that may be useful for reducing generalized anxiety and managing stress is breathing retraining. This method has not been studied for the treatment of SAD, though it is sometimes included as a component of treatment for panic disorder (e.g., Antony & McCabe, 2004). If this strategy is to be used in the treatment of a phobic disorder, including SAD, it is important that it be used primarily as a method of managing generalized anxiety (e.g., day-to-day worries about work, school, family, etc.), and not as a strategy for avoiding anxiety provoking sensations that are associated with exposure to social situations (e.g., preventing a panic attack at a meeting). Using breathing retraining as a safety behavior or avoidance strategy may undermine the effects of cognitive therapy and exposure, which are designed to help the individual to become more accepting of his or her feelings of anxiety and to confront anxiety provoking situations rather than avoid them. Breathing retraining involves learning to slow down one's breathing to a rate of about 3 or 4 seconds for each inhalation and 3 to 4 seconds for each exhalation. Individuals are encouraged to breathe using their diaphragm rather than their intercostal muscles (diaphragmatic breathing involves filling the lower parts of the lungs, whereas intercostal breathing tends to expand the upper parts of the chest). Clients are also taught to breathe through their noses, and to focus on becoming more relaxed using a meditation component during the breathing exercises.

4.2   Mechanisms of Action

Theories regarding the mechanisms underlying the effectiveness of cognitive behavioral treatments for SAD have ranged from cognitive explanations to behavioral theories and models involving emotional processing.

4.2.1   Cognitive Models

As reviewed in Chapter 2, cognitive models of SAD assume that social anxiety stems from a tendency to misinterpret social situations as dangerous and to engage in safety and avoidance behaviors that help to maintain the fear and anxiety over time by preventing the individual from learning that his or her anxiety provoking assumptions are untrue (Clark & Wells, 1995; Rapee & Heimberg, 1997). People with SAD tend to believe that it is very important to make a positive impression on others, that they are unlikely to make a positive impression, and that the consequences of not making a positive impression will be disastrous. Cognitive strategies are designed to help individuals to shift their anxiety provoking thinking patterns by examining the evidence for these beliefs, discounting unrealistic beliefs based on the evidence, and replacing anxiety provoking thoughts with more realistic and balanced beliefs and predictions.

Exposure-based strategies can also be understood from a cognitive perspective (Antony & Roemer, 2003; Moscovitch et al., in press). For example, Mineka and Thomas (1999) suggested that exposure therapy reduces anxiety by disconfirming a client's beliefs that he or she has little or no control over anxiety provoking situations. Other investigators (e.g., Rachman, 1996; Zinbarg, 1993) have suggested that exposure therapy provides clients with new experiences that challenge previous beliefs that feared situations are dangerous, which in turn lead them to spend more time in these situations, thereby further disconfirming their anxious predictions. Despite these suggestions, and the fact that many cognitive behavioral therapists assume that exposure works by altering anxiety provoking cognitions, there remains little clear evidence for this assumption.

4.2.2   Behavioral Models

A number of behavioral theories have been used to explain the effects of CBT, and particularly the effects of exposure-based treatments, as well as social skills training. These include constructs such as habituation, extinction, and reinforcement-based approaches.

Habituation is frequently mentioned in the CBT literature as a possible mechanism underlying the effects of exposure. Habituation is a natural, universal perceptual process that leads to a reduced response to a stimulus over time. It is also associated with a reinstatement of the response after a break from the stimulus. For example, when first entering a room with fresh cut flowers, a person would likely be very aware of the smell the flowers, but gradually would get used to the flowers and stop being aware of the smell. However, after leaving the room and returning, the individual's awareness of the smell of the flowers returns. As reviewed by Moscovitch et al. (in press), the notion of habituation does not adequately explain the effects of exposure, in part because individuals do not always experience reduction in fear during exposure, and because complete reinstatement of fear in between sessions usually does not occur. In fact, most clients experience a reduction in fear across sessions. Finally, habituation is an automatic perceptual process, rather than one involving new learning. Yet it is well established that fear reduction following exposure does involve new learning (Moscovitch et al., in press).

An alternate behavioral explanation for the effects of exposure involves extinction learning. According to Pavlovian conditioning theory, extinction is defined as a decrease in responding that occurs when a conditioned stimulus is presented repeatedly in the absence of an unconditioned stimulus (e.g., when an individual repeatedly engages in public speaking, and discovers that there are no negative consequences). Extinction does not involve unlearning of a previously learned association; rather, it is believed to be an active learning process in which people come to associate safety with a previously feared situation (Rescorla, 2001). As reviewed by Moscovitch et al. (in press), an extinction model appears to fit the data regarding the effects of exposure better than a habituation model. Furthermore, an extinction model is not necessarily incompatible with a cognitive understanding of the mechanisms underlying exposure. It is widely believed that cognitive factors such as information processing are involved in extinction learning.

Finally, some behavioral models assume that problem behaviors are a function of environmental contingencies. In other words, they persist over time because they are reinforced by the individual's environment. For example, avoidance of feared social situations persists over time because of negative reinforcement associated with the relief that the individual experiences when he or she escapes from the feared situation. By deciding to stay in a feared situation, rather than escaping, the individual prevents the sudden and powerful experience of relief, thereby breaking the cycle of avoidance and the associated negative reinforcement.

The effects of social skills training can also be understood from within an operant conditioning framework. As individuals improve their social skills, presumably others will begin to respond more favorably to them, thereby reinforcing individuals' attempts to use more appropriate social behaviors.

4.2.3   Emotional Processing Models

Emotional processing theories are based on the assumption that fear is represented as a networked memory structure containing three types of information: (a) information about a feared object or situation (e.g., a party), (b) information about one's responses to the feared stimulus (e.g., avoidance, sweating, etc.), and (c) information about the meaning of the feared stimulus and fear responses (e.g., the assumption that sweating at a party is threatening). In their classic emotional processing model, Foa and Kozak (1986) proposed that altering an emotional memory requires activation of the fear network and encoding of new information that is incompatible with the information originally stored in emotional memory. Exposure-based treatments are believed to be effective because they activate an individual's associative fear network (including stimulus, response, and meaning elements of the fear), and incorporate new, nonthreatening information into the network.

According to emotional processing models, exposure therapy can only lead to fear reduction across time if the client's fear is activated during practices

4.3   Efficacy

This section includes a summary of the research regarding the efficacy of CBT for SAD, including a description of studies investigating CBT and its components and predictors of outcome. Although there are no data concerning predictors of relapse or strategies for preventing relapse or recurrence, clinical suggestions are provided regarding this issue.

4.3.1   Efficacy of CBT

Numerous studies have found cognitive and behavioral techniques to be effective for reducing symptoms of SAD

Numerous studies have demonstrated that CBT is an effective treatment for SAD (for recent reviews, see Magee, Erwin, & Heimberg, in press; Rodebaugh et al., 2004). Typically, treatments include various combinations of exposure-based strategies, cognitive therapy, social skills training, and applied relaxation. They may be delivered in a group or individual format, and generally both of theses approaches seem to be effective. For example, group CBT (including exposure and cognitive therapy) has been found to be more effective than supportive psychotherapy (Heimberg et al., 1990), and improvements have been found to be maintained for up to 5 years (Heimberg, Salzman, Holt, & Blendell, 1993). Similarly, in a study of individual treatment (including exposure and social skills training), Turner et al. (1994) found that 84% of individuals met criteria for high or moderate end-state functioning following treatment.

Comparing CBT Components and Formats

There is considerable literature regarding the relative and combined effects of various CBT components, including exposure, cognitive therapy, social skills training, and applied relaxation. Studies have also compared various CBT formats (e.g., group versus individual therapy).

In vivo exposure and cognitive therapy. In vivo exposure alone has been found to be more effective than progressive muscle relaxation (Al-Kubaisny et al., 1992), pill placebo (Turner, Beidel, & Jacob, 1994), and a wait-list control condition (Newman, Hofmann, Trabert, Roth, & Taylor, 1994). Whereas some studies have found that adding cognitive strategies to exposure leads to improved outcomes relative to exposure alone (e.g., Mattick & Peters, 1988; Mattick, Peters, & Clarke, 1989), other studies have found little benefit of combining cognitive strategies with exposure (e.g., Mersch, 1995; Scholing & Emmelkamp, 1993). Nevertheless, adding cognitive strategies to exposure may have additional benefits, including improved maintenance of gains during follow-up, and a reduction in the amount of exposure necessary to achieve the same degree of improvement (Magee et al., in press). In addition, there is clear evidence that the combination of these approaches is more effective than supportive psychotherapy (Heimberg et al., 1990), pill placebo (Heimberg et al., 1998), and wait-list control conditions (Hope, Heimberg, & Bruch, 1995).

Social skills training. Although there is little evidence from controlled studies to support the use of social skills training alone as a treatment for SAD (for a review, see Magee et al., in press), a recent study suggests that social skills training may lead to enhanced outcomes when added to other CBT strategies (e.g., cognitive restructuring and exposure), compared to these strategies without social skills training (Herbert et al., 2005).

Relaxation training. Progressive muscle relaxation alone is not particularly useful for the treatment of SAD (Al-Kubaisy et al., 1992), though when it is combined with graduated exposure to feared situations (i.e., applied relaxation), it has been shown to be more effective than a wait list control condition (Jerremalm, Jansson, & Öst, 1986). However, there is also evidence that applied relaxation may be less effective than cognitive treatment (e.g., Jerremalm et al., 1986), even when combined with a traditional exposure-based treatment (Clark et al., 2006).

Findings from meta-analyses. Five major meta-analyses have attempted to answer the question of which treatment components are most effective for treating SAD (Chambless & Hope, 1996; Federoff & Taylor, 2001; Feske & Chambless, 1995; Gould, Buckminster, Pollack, Otto, & Yap, 1997; Taylor, 1996). Across meta-analyses, all of these strategies have been found to have moderate to large effect sizes in comparison to wait-list control conditions (Rodebaugh et al., 2004). However, these meta-analytic studies differ with respect to the question of whether cognitive restructuring plus exposure is

Table 13
Effects of CBT for Social Anxiety Disorder in Selected Studies

Study	Conditions	Effect Sizes (Cohen's d)	% Responders	Comments
Clark et al., 2006	Cognitive therapy	2.63	84%	Up to 14 weekly sessions. Effect sizes were based on post treatment scores on a composite of measures, in comparison to those in the wait list condition. Responder status refers to the number of participants no longer meeting criteria for SAD at posttreatment. CT was superior to exposure + AR.
	Exposure + AR	1.46	46%	
	Wait list	–	0%	
Davidson et al., 2004	FLU	1.52	50.9%	14 weeks of treatment. Estimates based on pre- to posttreatment changes on the CGI Scale (intent to treat sample). All active treatments equally effective, and more effective than placebo.
	CCBT	1.81	51.7%	
	CCBT/FLU	1.54	54.2%	
	CCBT/PBO	1.65	50.8%	
	PBO	0.94	31.9%	
Heimberg et al., 1998	CBGT	1.83	75%	12 weeks of treatment. Estimates based on pre- to posttreatment changes on the Social Phobic Disorders Severity and Change Form (completers only). CBGT equal to phenelzine, both of which superior to the other conditions.
	Phenelzine	1.82	77%	
	Pill placebo	1.09	41%	
	Supportive therapy	.97	35%	
Herbert et al., 2004	CBT over 12 weeks	1.25 (week 18)	67% (week 18)	12 sessions of CBT provided over 12 weekly sessions or over 18 weeks. Estimates based on changes on the SPAI-SP (intent to treat sample). For completers, standard 12 week CBT superior to extended CBT at week 12, but not at week 18. Over 85% of completers in both groups were responders.
	CBT over 18 weeks	0.64 (week 18)	42% (week 18)	
Herbert et al., 2005	CBGT with SST	1.90	79%	12 sessions of CBGT. Estimates based on pre- to posttreatment changes on the SPAI-SP. CBGT with SST significantly better than CBGT alone.
	CBGT without SST	0.62	38%	

Study	Conditions	Effect Sizes (Cohen's *d*)	% Responders	Comments
Hope et al., 1995	CBGT Exposure only Wait list	.85 1.27 −.21	36.4% 70% 0%	12 weekly sessions of group treatment. Effect size estimates based on pre- to posttreatment changes on the FQ-Social Phobia scale (completers only). Responder status based on the Clinician's Severity Rating. Overall, both treatment conditions were more effective than wait list, with CBGT being superior, inferior, or equivalent to exposure, depending on the measure.
Mattick et al., 1989	Exposure CR Exposure + CR Wait list	1.04 0.61 1.83 −.03	27% 45% 72% —	Treatment was in six group sessions. Effect size estimates based on pre- to posttreatment changes on the SPS (completers only). Responder status based on the percentage of individuals deemed to be highly improved or very highly improved on a composite of measures. Results varied by measure, but generally, CR was less effective than the other conditions, and Exposure + CR was the most effective condition.
Mörtberg et al., 2007	IGCT ICT TAU	.99 1.89 .58	26% 56% 24%	Effect size estimates based on pretreatment to 12-month response on a composite of measures (intent to treat sample). Responder status based on the percentage of individuals deemed to have obtained clinically significant improvement at posttreatment on a composite of measures. All treatments effective, with ICT being the most effective.
Turner et al., 1994	Flooding Atenolol Placebo	.94 .40 .75	55.6% 13.3% 6.3%	Treatment over 3 months (20 sessions). Estimates based on pre- to posttreatment changes on the SPAI-SP (completers only) for effect sizes. Responder status based on a composite of measures. Flooding included imaginal and in vivo exposure, and was superior to other treatments.

Note: AR = applied relaxation, CBT = cognitive behavioral therapy, CBGT = cognitive behavioral group therapy (cognitive restructuring, exposure), CCBT = comprehensive cognitive behavioral therapy (cognitive restructuring, exposure, social skills training), CGI = Clinical Global Impressions, CR = cognitive restructuring, FLU = fluoxetine, ICT = individual cognitive therapy (16 weekly sessions), IGCT = intensive group cognitive therapy (16 sessions over 3 weeks), PBO = placebo, FQ-Social Phobia = Fear Questionnaire (social phobia subscale), SPAI-SP = Social Phobia and Anxiety Inventory social phobia subscale, SPS = Social Phobia Scale, SST = social skills training, TAU = treatment as usual (an SSRI and therapy sessions as needed for 1 year. Cohen's *d* calculated based on formula presented by Cohen (1988), .20–.49 = small effect; .50–.79 = medium effect; .80 and above = large effect.

more effective then exposure alone. For example, Gould et al. (1997) found that exposure had the largest effect sizes of all the strategies (either when administered alone or with cognitive restructuring). Feske and Chambless (1995) found no differences between exposure alone and exposure combined with cognitive restructuring. Finally Taylor (1996) found that only treatments combining cognitive restructuring and exposure were more effective than placebo. Effect sizes for cognitive restructuring alone, exposure alone, and social skills training alone were equivalent to those for placebo in the analysis by Taylor.

Individual versus group treatment. Research on the relative effectiveness of group versus individual treatment for SAD has been equivocal. Stangier, Heidenreich, Peitz, Lauterbach, and Clark (2003) compared individual cognitive therapy and group cognitive therapy over 15 weekly sessions, and found individual therapy to be superior. Treatment was based on a protocol described by Clark and Wells (1995), including training in shifting attentional focus to external cues, stopping safety behaviors, video feedback to correct distorted self-imagery, behavioral experiments, and cognitive restructuring. Though the treatment was originally developed to be administered on an individual basis, it was adapted into a group format for the purpose of this study. The group treatment was not Heimberg's cognitive behavioral group therapy (Heimberg & Becker, 2002), which is the form of group treatment that has received the most support in the literature. Several unpublished studies using Heimberg's treatment have found no differences in the effectiveness of individual and group treatments (Lucas & Telch, 1993; Öst, Sedvall, Breitholz, Hellström, & Lindwall, 1995). Furthermore, meta-analyses have failed to find differences in the effectiveness of individual versus group therapies (Federoff & Taylor, 2001; Gould et al., 1997; Taylor, 1996).

Summary of selected controlled studies. Table 13 includes a summary of nine controlled studies comparing the various CBT components (e.g., cognitive restructuring, exposure, etc.), CBT formats (e.g., brief versus extended, group versus individual, intensive versus standard), or CBT to another treatment (e.g., medication, supportive psychotherapy). The studies included in the table were selected to be representative of a much larger literature on this topic. For each study, the table includes effect sizes and the percentage of participants deemed to have responded to each treatment condition.

4.3.2　Predictors of Outcome

Ledley and Heimberg (2005) reviewed the literature on predictors of outcome in the treatment of SAD. Two variables that have been examined as possible predictors include SAD subtype and presence of avoidant personality disorder, both of which are also related to the symptom severity. With respect to subtype, there is evidence that individuals with generalized SAD improved to the same extent as individuals with nongeneralized SAD (Brown, Heimberg, & Juster, 1995). However, because generalized SAD is associated with greater impairment at the beginning of treatment, fewer individuals from the generalized subtype achieve a high level of end-state functioning by the end of treatment. The presence of avoidant personality disorder has been found to interfere with treatment in some studies (see Ledley & Heimberg, 2005); however, when subtype of SAD is taken into account, the presence of avoidant personality disorder appears to be unrelated to outcome (Brown et al., 1995). This result may be due to the strong relationship between avoidant personality disorder and generalized SAD.

A number of other variables have been studied as possible predictors of treatment outcome in individuals with SAD, including comorbid depression, comorbid anger, treatment expectancies, and homework compliance (for a review, see Ledley & Heimberg, 2005). The effects of comorbid depression on outcome have been mixed, with some studies finding that depression interferes with treatment of SAD (Chambless, Tran, & Glass, 1997), and others finding that comorbid depression does not impact upon the outcome (Erwin et al., 2002). Erwin, Heimberg, Schneier, and Liebowitz (2003) found that problems with anger predicted drop out from a 12-session group CBT treatment for SAD, as well as a poorer treatment response among those who completed treatment.

Finally, various process variables have been found to impact upon treatment. Two studies (Chambless et al., 1997; Safren, Heimberg, & Juster, 1997) found that clients who expected a more positive outcome from CBT tended to do better during treatment. Similarly, compliance with CBT homework has been found to predict outcome in several studies (e.g., Edelman & Chambless, 1995; Leung & Heimberg, 1996). Increases in group cohesion (i.e., the extent to which group members feel supported by and affiliated with one another) over the course of group CBT have also been found to be related to be more positive outcome in one study (Taube-Schiff, Suvak, Antony, Bieling, & McCabe, 2007), though a previous study using a different measure of group cohesion (Woody & Adessky, 2002) found no relationship between group cohesion and treatment outcome.

> A client's expectations regarding treatment have been found to predict treatment outcome

4.3.3   Preventing Relapse and Return of Symptoms

Little has been written on predictors of relapse in the treatment of SAD. However, based on their clinical experience, Ledley and Heimberg (2005) suggest two variables that may contribute to relapse and recurrence of symptoms. The first is continued avoidance of social situations, and the second is a failure to generalize the treatment strategies and practices to new situations.

Preparation for termination should begin right at the first treatment session. Clients should be informed that treatment is unlikely to remove all of their social anxiety symptoms. Rather, the goal of treatment is to teach the client to be his or her own therapist, so that he or she can continue to work on the social anxiety even after treatment has ended. The exercises used during treatment should focus on helping the client to manage anxiety in the context of feared situations that arise in his or her daily life, and the client should be encouraged to apply the treatment strategies to new situations that arise after the end of treatment.

There are a number of specific methods that can be used to reduce the likelihood of relapse after successful treatment (Ledley & Heimberg, 2005). First, clients should have reasonable and realistic expectations regarding their functioning after treatment has terminated. Although most clients improve during treatment for SAD, many continue to struggle with occasional anxiety, and may still avoid some situations. Clients should be taught that it is normal to feel anxious in social situations from time to time. Efforts should be made to instill confidence in the client's ability to continue using the treatment strategies once treatment has ended. In particular, it may be useful for clients to continue to complete thought records from time to time, and to take advantage of exposure opportunities when they arise. Periodically, clients should take stock of where they are in their lives with respect to their social anxiety, and to examine their short-term, medium-term, and long-term goals. Regularly scheduled booster sessions, either in person or over the telephone, may also be useful to keep clients on track after treatment has ended. In addition, encouraging clients to become involved in activities that force them to have regular social contact is likely to be useful. For example, clients might attend regular meetings of Toastmasters, join a volleyball league, or become more active in their communities. Occasionally rereading relevant self-help books or joining a local anxiety support group may also be useful.

In short, prevention of relapse requires taking normal anxiety fluctuations in stride, continuing occasional exposures, continuing to challenge anxiety provoking thoughts, paying attention to one's goals, and seeking help before an increase in anxiety becomes a significant problem. Maintenance medications may also help prevent recurrence of symptoms for some individuals.

4.4   Combination Treatments

Pharmacotherapy is an effective treatment for SAD, either alone or in combination with CBT. This section reviews the use of medication treatments for SAD, followed by a review of studies examining the relative and combined effects of pharmacotherapy and CBT (i.e., cognitive strategies and/or behavioral strategies) for this condition.

4.4.1   Medication Treatments

SSRI antidepressants and venlafaxine are the medications treatments of choice for SAD

Table 5 (Chapter 3) provides a list of evidence-based medication treatments for SAD, including recommended initial and maximum dosages. A wide range of antidepressants has been found to be effective for treating SAD, including selective serotonin reuptake inhibitors (SSRIs; e.g., citalopram, escitalopram, fluoxetine, fluvoxamine, paroxetine, sertraline), monoamine oxidase inhibitors (e.g., phenelzine), and serotonin norepinephrine reuptake inhibitors (e.g., venlafaxine XR) (Swinson et al., 2006). In contrast, tricyclic antidepressants such as imipramine do not appear to be effective for treating SAD (Simpson et al., 1998), though they are useful in the treatment of panic disorder (for a review, see Antony & Swinson, 2000). Certain benzodiazepines, such as clonazepam and alprazolam have been found to be useful for treating SAD, and there is also evidence supporting the use of gabapentin, an anticonvulsant (Swinson et al., 2006).

A detailed review of the evidence supporting these and other medications is available in the Canadian Psychiatric Association's *Clinical Practice Guidelines for the Management of Anxiety Disorders* (Swinson et al., 2006). These guidelines can be downloaded from: (http://ww1.cpa-apc.org:8080/Publications/CJP/supplements/july2006/anxiety_guidelines_2006.pdf).

Medications approved by the United States Food and Drug Administration for the treatment of SAD include paroxetine, paroxetine controlled-release, sertraline, and venlafaxine. Despite its effectiveness, phenelzine is rarely used to treat this disorder because of potentially severe side effects, frequent interactions with other medications, and strict dietary restrictions (foods containing tyramine, including certain cured meats, cheeses, and wines, for example, must be avoided). SSRIs and venlafaxine are typically considered to be first-line treatments for this condition, and are usually well-tolerated by clients. Commonly reported side effects include gastrointestinal symptoms, sleep disturbance, and headache, and these often improve over time. In some clients, symptoms of agitation, tremor, and anxiety may occur early in treatment, and also tend to improve over time. These symptoms can be managed by starting at lower dosages and increasing dosages gradually. Weight gain and sexual side effects are also common, and these symptoms often continue over the course of treatment. Most SSRIs and venlafaxine are usually easy to discontinue, though paroxetine discontinuation is often associated with "flu-like" withdrawal symptoms due to its short half-life. Therefore, it is important to discontinue paroxetine more gradually than might be the case for other SSRIs.

Benzodiazepines may be an option for individuals who have difficulty tolerating antidepressants, as well as for individuals taking medication as needed or on a "prn" basis. Though antidepressants typically take several weeks to have an effect, the therapeutic effects of benzodiazepines are usually experienced within an hour or less. The most common side effects of benzodiazepines include sedation, physical changes (e.g., changes in balance), and cognitive impairment (e.g., memory impairments). Because of concerns about possible dependency, benzodiazepines should usually be restricted to short-term use, and should be used with great caution in older adults and individuals with a history of substance abuse. Discontinuation of benzodiazepines should be completed at a gradual pace to minimize withdrawal symptoms.

4.4.2 Comparing and Combining Medications and CBT

This section reviews the relative and combined effects of medication and CBT for SAD. Although there are differences among individual studies with respect to the effectiveness of these particular treatments, summarizing across studies suggests that pharmacotherapy, CBT, and their combination are about equally effective for the treatment of SAD, particularly in the short term. Follow-up findings suggest that psychological treatments are less susceptible to relapse and recurrence relative to medication treatments, though more long-term studies are needed. Note that in each of the studies examining the effects of combination treatments, pharmacotherapy and CBT are introduced simultaneously. There are currently no studies examining the effects of delivering these treatments sequentially.

Over the long term, gains following CBT tend to be better maintained than gains obtained through pharmacotherapy, particularly after the medication has been discontinued

CBT Versus SSRIs

Rosser, Erskine, and Crino (2004) reported on findings from a naturalistic study in which individuals taking antidepressants responded to CBT no more or no less than did people who were not taking antidepressants. However, this study did not specify which antidepressants were being used by participants; nor were participants randomly assigned to the antidepressant and nonantidepressant conditions. Mörtberg, Clark, Sundin, Åberg, and Wistedt (2007) compared intensive group cognitive therapy, individual cognitive therapy, and treatment as usual with an SSRI for individuals suffering from SAD. In this study, all three conditions were found to be effective, with the largest changes occurring in the individual cognitive therapy condition, and no differences between the other two conditions.

In a 24-week, primary care study comparing sertraline, exposure therapy, and their combination, Blomhoff et al. (2001) randomly assigned individuals with SAD to receive either sertraline or placebo, combined with either exposure or general medical care. Participants who were treated with sertraline generally did better than those who were treated without sertraline. In addition, individuals who were treated with exposure generally did no better than those who were treated without exposure. Only the sertraline and the sertraline plus exposure conditions were more effective than placebo. However, during the one-year follow up period, individuals who received exposure continued improving, whereas there was deterioration in progress in the sertraline and the sertraline plus exposure conditions (Haug et al., 2003). One potential problem with this study is that treatment was provided by family physicians who were trained over the course of only three weekends, and who in many cases may have had no other experience or training in administering exposure therapy.

In a study investigating the relative and combined effects of cognitive therapy and fluoxetine, participants were randomly assigned to receive cognitive therapy alone, fluoxetine plus self-administered exposure assignments, or placebo plus self-administered exposure (Clark et al., 2003). Although all three conditions led to significant improvements, cognitive therapy was superior to the other two conditions following treatment, as well as at 12-month follow-up. There were no differences in effectiveness between the fluoxetine plus exposure condition and the placebo plus exposure condition.

In the largest study to date comparing pharmacotherapy, CBT, and their combination, Davidson et al. (2004) compared fluoxetine, comprehensive cognitive behavioral group therapy (CCBT), placebo, CCBT plus fluoxetine, and CCBT plus placebo. Treatment lasted 14 weeks. All four active treatments were more effective than placebo, and there were no differences among them. In other words, there was no benefit of combining CBT and pharmacotherapy over either treatment alone.

In summary, some studies have found some advantage for SSRI treatment over treatment with CBT (e.g., Blomhoff et al., 2001). Others have found an advantage for CBT (e.g., Clark et al., 2003). However, the largest study to date (Davidson et al., 2004) found no advantage of either psychological or pharmacological treatment, or their combination. Although it seems clear that SSRIs, CBT, and their combination are all effective options for individuals with SAD, it is still difficult to predict which approach is most likely to work for any particular individual. Future studies will need to examine the question of which treatments work best for which individuals.

CBT Versus MAOIs

Heimberg, Leibowitz, and colleagues have conducted a number of studies examining the relative and combined effects of phenelzine and cognitive behavioral group therapy (CBGT). Heimberg et al. (1998) compared CBGT, phenelzine, pill placebo, and a credible psychological placebo condition in a 12-week treatment study. Overall, CBGT and phenelzine were associated with equivalent response rates (75% and 77%, respectively), and both of these conditions were significantly more effective than the placebo conditions. Phenelzine was superior to CBGT on several measures, and led to more rapid improvements. However, following a six-month maintenance phase and a six-month follow-up phase, relapse rates were considerably higher in the phenelzine condition (50%) than the CBGT condition (17%) (Liebowitz et al., 1999). Preliminary data from a subsequent study suggest that the combination of phenelzine plus CBGT is more likely to be superior to pill placebo than either treatment alone (Heimberg, 2002).

Two studies have also compared CBT to moclobemide, a reversible MAOI that has milder side effects and a lack of dietary restrictions, relative to traditional MAOIs. Moclobemide has been found to be more effective than placebo in some studies of SAD, though evidence has been mixed (Swinson et al., 2006). Moclobemide is not available in the United States, though it is available in various other countries around the world.

Oosterbaan, van Balkom, Spinhoven, van Oppen, and van Dyck (2001) found that cognitive therapy was superior to moclobemide and placebo at two-month follow-up, and moclobemide did not differ from placebo. In another study (Prasko et al., 2006), CBT, moclobemide, and their combination were compared during a six-month treatment phase and again at 24-month follow-up. Combined CBT and moclobemide led to the most rapid changes. During the first three months of treatment, moclobemide was superior to CBT for the reduction of generalized anxiety, whereas CBT led to the largest improvement in avoidance behavior. After six months of treatment, groups receiving CBT achieved the best results, and there was no benefit of combining moclobemide with CBT. Relapse rates were lowest at 24-month follow-up in the CBT group compared to the group that received moclobemide alone.

CBT Versus Benzodiazepines

Two studies have compared benzodiazepine treatment to CBT for SAD. Gelernter et al. (1991) compared CBGT to pharmacotherapy with alprazolam, pharmacotherapy with phenelzine, or treatment with a pill placebo. All groups also received instructions to expose themselves to phobic stimuli. All four conditions showed significant improvement. Although phenelzine was found to be superior to alprazolam and placebo on a measure of social and work disability, few differences between conditions emerged overall. The lack of differences across conditions may have been related to the fact that self-exposure instructions were included in all four conditions. In a second study, Otto et al. (2000) found that CBGT and clonazepam were both effective treatments for SAD. On most measures, the two treatments were equivalent, though on several measures clonazepam was superior to CBT. In light of findings from other anxiety disorders that CBT is associated with lower rates of relapse relative to treatment with benzodiazepines (e.g., Marks et al., 1993), long term follow-up studies are needed.

Augmentation of Exposure with D-Cycloserine

D-cycloserine is an agonist of the glutamatergic N-methyl-d-aspartate receptor that traditionally has been used to treat tuberculosis, and has also been found to facilitate extinction learning in animals. Recently, there has been strong interest in d-cycloserine as a possible enhancer of the effects of exposure therapy for phobias. Hofmann et al. (2006) compared exposure therapy plus d-cycloserine versus exposure therapy plus placebo over five sessions of treatment. The medication or placebo was taken about one hour before each exposure session, which occurred during Sessions 2 through 5. Participants receiving d-cycloserine plus exposure reported significantly greater reductions in social anxiety than those who received exposure therapy plus placebo. Though this study remains to be replicated, these initial findings suggest that d-cycloserine may be useful for enhancing the effects of exposure. However, unlike other medications used to treat social anxiety, d-cycloserine is not an anxiolytic. On its own, this drug has little to no effect on anxiety. Rather, d-cycloserine is believed to work by enhancing learning, and therefore it has been studied only in the context of exposure-based treatments.

> **Preliminary studies suggest that d-cycloserine combined with exposure therapy may lead to better outcomes than exposure alone**

4.5   Overcoming Barriers to Treatment

Sections 4.1.3 and 4.1.4 include suggestions for overcoming obstacles that occur in the context of cognitive therapy and exposure-based strategies, respectively. This section focuses on more general barriers to treatment, including ambivalence about treatment, homework noncompliance, and the impact of comorbidity.

4.5.1   Treatment Ambivalence

Clients often have mixed feelings about receiving CBT. A study from our center on individuals with various anxiety disorders found that 92% of individuals with SAD reported concerns about starting treatment (Gifford, Purdon, Rowa, Young, & Antony, 2005). In general, these concerns fell into four main categories, including (a) fears that treatment will fail (e.g., "I am a hopeless case"), (b) fears regarding the consequences of treatment succeeding (e.g., "others will be more demanding of me if I get better"), (c) fears that treatment will lead to an increase in symptoms (e.g., "I will develop a new irrational fear"), and (d) other general concerns (e.g., "treatment will interfere with work," "my therapist will think badly of me"). The most common concerns reported by individuals with SAD fell into the first (treatment will fail) and fourth (general concerns) categories.

There are a number of approaches to dealing with ambivalence about treatment. One strategy is to identify cognitive and behavioral factors that contribute to ambivalence, and to target these using CBT strategies. For example, a client who is convinced that treatment will fail might be encouraged to examine the evidence for and against this belief. Similarly, a client who is worried about treatment interfering with other responsibilities at home or at work might be encouraged to use problem solving and time management strategies to identify ways of completing treatment while meeting these responsibilities.

Perhaps the best known method for dealing with treatment ambivalence is a set of procedures collectively known as *motivational interviewing* (Miller & Rollnick, 2002). Motivational interviewing may be defined as a "client-centered, directive method for enhancing intrinsic motivation to change by exploring and resolving ambivalence" (Miller & Rollnick, 2002). It has been studied most frequently in people with substance use disorders and people who are medically ill and are reluctant to make lifestyle changes (e.g., exercise, diet, medication compliance, etc.). Some of the key assumptions of motivational interviewing include the following:

- Motivational interviewing is an approach to prepare a client for treatment, and is therefore complementary to CBT.
- People are often ambivalent about change. For example, although a client may recognize that avoidance of social situations limits opportunities, he or she may also be aware that avoidance prevents the rejection that sometimes occurs when social risks are taken.
- Motivation is viewed as occurring in an interpersonal context, rather than residing in the individual. Resistance is a product of ambivalence, and occurs in the context of the interaction between the client and therapist. It is a sign of a problem in the therapeutic relationship, rather than a sign of the client simply being uncooperative.
- To benefit from treatment, the client must be *willing*, *able*, and *ready* to change. In other words, the client must believe that change is an important priority, and that he or she will be able to change, once provided with the right tools.
- The focus of motivational interviewing is on intrinsic reasons for change (e.g., changes that are consistent with the client's personal values), rather than on extrinsic reasons (e.g., financial gains, social pressure, etc.).

In motivational interviewing, the therapist is encouraged to reduce behaviors that are likely to increase client resistance. These include arguing for change, assuming an expert role, accepting diagnostic labels as an explanation of the client's behavior, and being in a hurry for the client to change. Instead, the therapist highlights and amplifies the discrepancy between the client's values and goals on the one hand, and his or her current behavior on the other hand. The therapist expresses empathy, supports the client's efforts to develop self-efficacy, and encourages the client to generate intrinsic reasons for change. The therapist *rolls with resistance*, rather than targeting resistance directly or advocating for change, which are believed to amplify resistance.

To date, only one study has investigated the use of motivational interviewing in the treatment of individuals with anxiety disorders. Westra and Dozois (2006) studied 55 participants with SAD, panic disorder, or GAD. Individuals received either three sessions of motivational interviewing or no pretreatment sessions prior to receiving group CBT. Motivational interviewing was associ-

Motivational enhancement strategies may be useful for clients who are ambivalent about treatment

ated with a stronger response to treatment, as well as greater compliance with homework. Despite several methodological limitations, the results of the study are encouraging.

A thorough consideration of motivational interviewing is beyond the scope of this discussion. Several other sources are available for the interested reader (e.g., Arkowitz, Westra, Miller, & Rollnick, 2008; Miller & Rollnick, 2002).

4.5.2   Homework Noncompliance

As reviewed earlier, several studies have found homework compliance to be correlated with a more positive outcome following CBT. Homework helps to reinforce the strategies learned during therapy sessions, and facilitates the generalization of skills to naturalistic settings and situations that often cannot be targeted within the treatment session (e.g., exposure practices at work, at parties, or in other social situations).

Improving homework compliance depends on first being able to identify the reasons why a client is not completing homework. Possible reasons for homework noncompliance may include (a) not understanding the task (e.g., a complex monitoring form may be difficult to understand, particularly a few days after it is first explained during the treatment session); (b) homework assignments that are not relevant to the client (e.g., an assignment to talk to other people at a bar may not seem relevant to a client has no interest in becoming more comfortable in bars); (c) homework tasks that are too frightening; (d) interpersonal issues (e.g., problems in the therapeutic relationship); (e) other demands on the client's time (e.g., busy work schedule, family responsibilities); and (f) failure of the therapist to ask about homework at the beginning of each session.

Once the reasons for homework noncompliance have been identified, attempts can be made to improve compliance by targeting the specific issue. For instance, if a client's noncompliance is related to homework complexity, it may be useful to simplify homework assignments by reducing the variety of exposure practices in a given week, or by simplifying cognitive monitoring forms, for example. Providing homework instructions in writing may also be helpful, and illustrating homework practices in session first will ensure that the client understands what is expected when he or she attempts the practice for homework.

In the case of exposure homework, noncompliance is often due to fear. Even in cases where the client was able to enter a situation during a therapy session, repeating the practice for homework, without the therapist present, may be difficult. If a practice is too difficult, the therapist should assign less frightening homework practices. Scheduling telephone contacts between sessions may also be helpful. Clients often leave a therapy session feeling confident about being able to complete homework; however, over the next few days, confidence may fade. A short phone call may help to boost the client's confidence to the point that homework can be completed.

If lack of compliance appears to be related to poor organization, scheduling conflicts, or demands on the client's time, a problem-solving approach may be useful for improving homework completion. Key steps include identifying barriers to homework completion, brainstorming possible solutions, evaluating each potential solution, selecting the best solution, and finally, implementing the selected solution. For example, a client who is having difficulty finding time to socialize with others may try combining social activities with other tasks and activities that he or she is already engaged in (e.g., eating with others instead of eating alone).

If homework compliance continues to be a problem, scheduling treatment sessions more frequently may reduce the need for homework. For example, if the client and therapist are able to meet several times per week, and to practice exposure and cognitive strategies during each of those meetings, a significant reduction in anxiety may occur even if the client does not practice exposure between sessions. Another option is to combine homework assignments with brief visits with the therapist. For example, the client and therapist might arrange to meet for a few minutes or have brief phone contact before and after the client spends an hour our two completing an exposure practice at a nearby mall.

In some cases, a lack of homework compliance may indicate poor motivation for treatment. For these clients, motivational enhancement strategies may be useful, as discussed in the previous section. Finally, arriving at a mutual decision to take a break from therapy may sometimes be appropriate, particularly for clients who are clearly not invested in the treatment.

4.5.3   Adapting Treatment for Comorbidity

As reviewed in Chapter 1, many people with SAD present with a number of different additional problems, including other anxiety disorders, depression, substance use disorders, or other psychological disorders. There is little to no research regarding the best ways to treat SAD in the context of other disorders. However, there have been studies examining the impact of comorbidity on the treatment of SAD. Comorbidity with other anxiety disorders does not appear to affect outcome of treatment for SAD (for a review, see Magee et al., in press), though studies on the impact of depression on SAD treatment have yielded mixed results. As reviewed earlier, some studies have found that comorbid depression leads to worse outcomes during CBT for SAD, and other studies have found that depression does not have an impact on outcome. Research on the relationship between comorbid personality disorders and outcome of CBT for SAD has also been mixed (Magee et al., in press), though most of these studies examined only comorbidity with avoidant personality disorder, and little is known about the impact of other personality disorders on outcome. Researchers have generally not studied the impact of substance use disorders on the treatment of SAD, though clinical experience suggests that individuals with SAD who abuse substances may be more challenging to treat.

For individuals who have comorbid anxiety disorders, treatment may focus first on the most significant problem (i.e., the one causing the greatest distress and impairment; the one for which the client wants to be treated), followed by treatment of any additional anxiety disorders later. However, an alternative is to treat the various anxiety disorders concurrently. There is evidence that a unified anxiety disorders treatment can be used effectively for people with a wide range of anxiety disorder diagnoses (Norton, in press).

Because the strategies used to treat these conditions are very similar, and the boundaries between anxiety disorders are often blurred (e.g., most of the anxiety disorders are associated with discomfort in social situations, though perhaps for different reasons), it is often possible to treat multiple anxiety disorders at the same time. For example, an individual with both panic disorder and SAD might practice exposure to both social situations and agoraphobic situations, practice exposure to feared sensations in both social situations and nonsocial situations, and challenge anxiety provoking thoughts related to both social threat and panic-related threat.

For individuals with other types of comorbidity (e.g., substance use disorders, personality disorders), it is important to assess the relative severity of the individual's SAD and other disorders. If the other conditions are milder and somewhat under control, it may be possible to focus on the SAD without much attention to the other conditions. In cases where the other disorders are severe, and their symptoms are likely to have an impact on the treatment of SAD, it may be necessary to treat the other condition first, or to treat the SAD and other conditions concurrently. Concurrent treatment makes the most sense when the SAD and other conditions appear to be functionally related. For example, a client who drinks excessively because of social anxiety might not respond well to a treatment that focuses exclusively on the social anxiety or on the alcohol use. Rather, an integrated treatment that targets the core features of both problems might be best.

> **Generally, there is little research on the best ways to treat people who have SAD as well as other comorbid problems**

A thorough discussion of how to treat the range of problems that can occur in the context of SAD is beyond the scope of this book. Instead, the reader is referred to sources that discuss the treatment of these specific disorders. An example is Barlow's *Clinical Handbook of Psychological Disorders*, which provides step-by-step protocols for treating a variety of problems (Barlow, 2008). A number of other excellent books discussing evidence-based treatments for particular psychological disorders are available, including those in the *Advances in Psychotherapy: Evidence-Based Practice* series from Hogrefe and Huber Publishers (http://www.hhpub.com), and the *Treatments that Work* series from Oxford University Press (http://www.oup.com/us).

4.6   Adapting Treatment for Different Age Groups

4.6.1   Children and Adolescents

SAD is a common problem in children, with prevalence estimates ranging from 1% to 13% (Furr, Tiwari, Suveg, & Kendall, in press). The basic strategies used to treat SAD in children and adolescents are similar to those used in the treatment of adults, including cognitive restructuring, exposure, and social skills training. However, when treating younger individuals, strategies are typically adapted to be age-appropriate. For example, instead of an exposure hierarchy, the metaphor of an *exposure stepladder* is often used, where each rung of the ladder represents an exposure step. In addition, because it is often difficult for children to appreciate the long-term benefits of conducting exposure practices, rewards are often used to reinforce completion of exposure practices and other treatment-related tasks. These may include stickers, money, toys, or special privileges at home (e.g., staying up late to watch a favorite television show), for instance. Another example of how treatment may be adapted for children is the use of a *fear thermometer* instead of the standard 0–100 numerical scale that adults use to rate their levels of fear. Children are asked to indicate their fear level during exposure practices by pointing to the appropriate location on a picture of a thermometer, in which the bottom of the thermometer indicates low levels of fear and a top of the thermometer indicates high levels of fear.

Cognitive tools may also need to be adapted for children. For example, thought records may need to be simplified, and the rationale for cognitive restructuring must be explained at an age-appropriate level. In very young children, it may be difficult to use cognitive strategies because the child may be unable to identify his or her anxiety provoking beliefs.

When treating children, it is common practice to include parents in the treatment. This is important because it is typically the parents who will ensure that treatment homework is completed between sessions. It is also useful for parents to learn strategies to stop any behaviors that may function to reinforce the child's anxiety or avoidance (e.g., allowing the child to stay home from school when feeling anxious). If a parent suffers from social anxiety, it may be helpful for that parent to seek treatment. Modeling nonfearful behavior in front of the anxious child may facilitate the child's recovery.

As with adults, children may be treated individually or in groups. It is not unusual in studies of anxious children to include a mixture of different anxiety disorders in the same group (e.g., Kendall et al., 1997). Once an adolescent reaches an age of 15 or 16, standard adult treatments are likely to be appropriate.

A number of excellent resources (for therapists and parents) exist on the treatment of anxiety disorders in children in general (e.g., Chorpita, 2007; Rapee, Spence, Cobham, & Wignall, 2000; Rapee, Wignall, Hudson, & Schniering, 2000), as well as books on treating SAD in particular (Albano & DiBartolo, 2007; Kearney, 2005; McHolm, Cunningham, & Vanier, 2005).

4.6.2   Older Adults

SAD has been found to have a lifetime prevalence of 6.6% among adults over 60 years of age in the United States (Kessler et al., 2005), and 4.94% for older adults in Canada (Cairney et al., 2007). Although these estimates are lower than those for general adult samples (Kessler et al., 2005), they suggest that SAD continues to be a significant problem as people age. Nevertheless, there are very few studies examining the treatment of anxiety disorders in older adults, and almost all of these have been focused on GAD.

One treatment study to include older adults with SAD (Schuurmans et al., 2006) compared CBT to sertraline (an SSRI) for a mixed sample of older adults with various anxiety disorders, including SAD, GAD, panic disorder, and agoraphobia. Generally, CBT was found to be effective, though the effect sizes for sertraline were stronger. Data on the outcome of treatment for specific anxiety disorders were not presented in this study, so it is impossible to know the effects of treatment on SAD, in particular. We are aware of no other published studies on CBT for SAD in older adults.

In treating older adults, several factors need to be taken into account (for a review, see Ayers, Thorp, & Wetherell, in press). First, medical comorbidity can complicate the assessment and treatment of anxiety in this population. Many of the physical symptoms of anxiety can look similar to symptoms of medical illness, so it is particularly important for the individual to have a thorough medical workup. Similarly, memory loss can make it difficult for some individuals to complete CBT assignments. A study by Mohlman et al. (2003) included memory aids and strategies such as between-session telephone calls to increase homework compliance in a study of older adults with GAD. Because this study found larger effect sizes than typical studies of CBT in older adults with GAD, it is possible that such aids can enhance treatment outcome in this population. Finally, it is important to recognize that aging is often associated with interpersonal losses (e.g., death of a spouse, loss of family members and close friends) that may cause social anxiety to suddenly become an important issue for the first time. In such cases, treatment should emphasize helping the client to develop the skills necessary for expanding his or her social circle.

4.7   Adapting Treatment for Different Cultures

SAD appears to occur across cultures (Weissman et al., 1996). Although presentations of SAD are often similar across ethnic groups, there are also culture-specific ways in which SAD may present. For example, as reviewed in Chapter 1, in Japan and other Eastern cultures, there exists a condition called *taijin kyofusho syndrome*, in which the individual has an intense fear that his or her body or its functions may be offensive or embarrassing to others. Taijin kyofusho syndrome and SAD both appear to involve social anxiety and avoidance of social situations, and they appear to respond to similar pharmacological and behavioral treatments (Asmal & Stein, in press).

Very little research exists regarding the issue of how or whether treatment should be adapted for particular cultures, though preliminary studies suggest that CBT is effective across a number of cultural groups. One study by Pina, Silverman, Fuentes, Kurtines, and Weems (2003) found that Hispanic-American youth with phobic and anxiety disorders responded to an exposure-based treatment to the same degree as European-American youth. Another study by Ferrell, Beidel, and Turner (2004) suggested that African-American and White preadolescent children with SAD have similar symptomatic presentations, and respond similarly to behavioral treatment. Although these preliminary results suggest that cognitive behavioral techniques appear to be effective across a number of ethnic and cultural groups, more research is needed to better understand the effect of culture on treatment outcome, and the ways in which treatment should be adapted for culturally diverse groups.

Therapists should become acquainted with the ways in which culture has an impact on symptoms that may otherwise be associated with SAD. For example, decreased eye contact may have different meanings in different cultures.

Similarly, cultural groups may differ with respect to the amount of personal space deemed appropriate, with members of some cultures tending to stand closer to one another relative to those in other cultures. So, whereas decreased eye contact and preferring more personal space may be signs of social anxiety in Western cultures, these behaviors may mean something different in other cultural groups. Different cultural groups may also respond differently to a therapist's tendency to be directive versus more client centered. Cultures may also vary with respect to gender differences in the avoidance of social situations or in the tendency to dress more modestly in public.

Despite the possibility of cultural differences in the presentation of anxiety and response to treatment, the therapist must also be careful not to allow cultural stereotypes to influence his or her judgments regarding a client's behavior. The therapist must constantly assess the extent to which particular behaviors are related to the client's culture, anxiety, or other factors.

5

Case Vignettes

This chapter describes two case examples of individuals with SAD, along with treatment plans and exposure hierarchies. Each client was treated with cognitive behavioral therapy (CBT) with a range of 6 to 20 sessions. Participants benefited from CBT techniques as evidenced by their subjective self-report, lowered scores on symptom questionnaires, increased exposure to feared situations, and changes on clinician-administered measures of SAD symptoms.

Case 1: Susan's Public Speaking Fears

Susan, a 31-year-old marketing executive, presented with a discrete fear of giving presentations, both to large groups as well as to her six-person team, at work meetings. Susan had been working at her firm for five years, and presented for treatment after she was passed over for a promotion she had been working toward for the previous year. Evaluations stated that a main reason for her lack of promotion included her difficulty participating in team meetings and avoidance of larger presentations. In a diagnostic assessment, Susan denied experiencing social anxiety outside of these situations and therefore a diagnosis of SAD (nongeneralized type) was assigned. Susan attended six sessions of individual CBT for her fears.

The first two sessions of CBT involved educating Susan about the cognitive behavioral model of social anxiety, identifying and challenging Susan's fearful thoughts and predictions about giving talks, identifying Susan's safety behaviors, and developing an exposure hierarchy. Susan quickly realized that she engaged in a number of safety behaviors that were likely contributing to her anxiety rather than reducing it. For example, Susan acknowledged rehearsing and memorizing what she might say while sitting in meetings, to the point that she did not follow the discussion in the meeting. She also purposely wore turtlenecks and high collared sweaters, to hide flushing that often happened on her chest and neck when she was nervous. Although these tops allowed her to feel more protected, they also made her even warmer in the tight space of her boardroom. Armed with the knowledge of how these strategies might not be helpful, Susan agreed to eliminate their use to the best of her ability.

Susan identified a number of fearful thoughts and predictions about talking at meetings and giving presentations. She revealed concerns that she would lose her train of thought, that she would not be able to answer questions, and that others would think she was stupid as a result. When examining these fears in therapy, Susan described some stressful presentations at school where she did lose her train of thought and felt very embarrassed. However, on further examination, Susan's therapist helped her examine whether her feared outcome was as catastrophic or likely as she was making it out to be.

Therapist: So, when you are asked to do a presentation at work, you think of those times at school when you lost your train of thought during a presentation. How many times did that happen?

Susan: Oh, probably at least two or three times.

Therapist: Did you ever give a presentation where you *didn't* lose your train of thought?

Susan: Well, yes. But probably only because I'd rehearsed the presentation so many times beforehand.

Therapist: Fair enough. How many times do you think you made it through a presentation *without* losing your train of thought?

Susan: A few. Maybe ten or so.

Therapist: What do you make of these numbers?

Susan: Well, I guess I had more times I didn't mess up than times I did. But those times I did lose my train of thought were horrible!

Therapist: What made them horrible?

Susan: You know – it's just so embarrassing to forget what you're saying.

Therapist: Did anyone say anything or do anything – like walk out? Did the teacher say anything?

Susan: No. But they were probably thinking that I'm a total idiot.

Therapist: What might you say to a close friend if she forgot what she was saying in a presentation?

Susan: I'd tell my friend not to worry about it – it happens all the time.

Therapist: Is there anything else people could be thinking about you when you lose your train of thought?

Susan: I guess some people might be thinking about their own presentations… or just daydreaming. Some people might feel bad for me.

Therapist: So there might be a number of things people could be thinking about or focusing on. By the way, how long did you pause before you started talking again?

Susan: It felt like forever. Maybe 5 or 10 seconds.

Therapist: And then what happened?

Susan: Then I looked at my notes and started again.

Therapist: Interesting. Let's summarize. So what you're saying is that you have had a number of experiences in which you gave a presentation and didn't lose your train of thought. During times when you did lose your place, the pause was a few seconds before you started up again. So if it were to happen again in a presentation at work, would it really be that horrible? Would you really stop and never talk again?

Susan: I guess not. Maybe it just feels like that in the moment.

Although Susan was not fully convinced that losing her train of thought would not be horrible, she began to question that assumption. This allowed her to be more open to the idea of exposure as both a way to get used to

Table 14
Susan's Exposure Hierarchy

Number	Item Description	Fear Rating (0–100)
1	Give speech to large group, answer questions.	100
2	Give speech with pauses.	95
3	Give speech, wearing v-neck top.	90
4	Lead team meeting.	75
5	Give speech to small group.	65
6	Make a point at a team meeting.	50
7	Ask question at a team meeting.	45

public speaking, to test out whether her prediction about losing her train of thought comes true, and to find out how horrible it would actually be if she were to forget what she was saying. Susan's exposure hierarchy is shown in Table 14.

Session 3 included Susan's first exposure. She decided to try giving a presentation about a topic she knew well to a small audience (i.e., the therapist and two other people who worked with the therapist). Her preparation was limited, as instructed by the therapist due to her tendency to overrehearse and memorize presentations. She challenged her fearful thoughts prior to beginning her speech and tried to focus on her more realistic thoughts while giving the presentation. She rated her initial fear level as 50 (out of 100), which fell to 30 by the end of her 20 minute presentation. For homework, she was asked to practice participating in her team meeting in small ways on a daily basis (e.g., purposely asking a question or making at least one comment during a meeting). She was also asked to practice giving a short speech to close friends at least three times over the week.

Sessions 4, 5, and 6 involved further exposures. Susan tried all items on her hierarchy, including giving a presentation to a larger audience, purposely pausing during her presentation to mimic losing her train of thought, and answering spontaneous questions from a panel of the therapist and clinic members. By purposely "losing her train of thought," Susan was able to experience her worst fear and learn that she could live through it. She also learned that she was more capable than she gave herself credit for, as she did not have any experiences of completely losing her train of thought while speaking.

Between Sessions 4, 5, and 6, Susan continued exposures to her feared situations for homework. She decided to practice contributing even more to her team meetings, and also challenged herself to wear tops that did not cover her neck. To her surprise, no one appeared to notice her flushing, and the more she began to believe that this was not as big a deal as she once thought, she began to pay less and less attention to her flushing. Further, Susan began to reap the rewards of her hard work with positive comments from the team leader about her ideas and contributions to the meetings. As Susan approached her final session, she decided to offer to give a presentation at work. Once again, Susan committed to limiting her preparation of this talk, omitting any memorization of the content. To her delight, she was able to give a solid presentation where her fear level decreased from a rating of 75 to a rating of 30 over the course of the talk. On the encouragement of her therapist, Susan made a point of focusing on her audience rather than focusing on her own physical feelings. She found it helpful to challenge herself to notice something about everyone's appearance to ensure her attention was externally focused (e.g., noticing the color of each person's top). After her presentation, Susan reported having to use her cognitive strategies to challenge some doubts about whether she really had done a good job, and whether people were bored. She focused on some positive feedback she had received, and thought of all the reasons why one of her colleagues might have left her presentation in the middle, instead of simply assuming he thought she was stupid.

Susan terminated therapy feeling more confident about her ability to give presentations and less worried about the consequences of making mistakes during presentations. To maintain her gains, she committed to leading weekly team meetings, a task that involved talking in front of her team as well as answering questions about a particular project.

Case 2: Jeremy's Generalized Social Fears

Jeremy was a 42-year-old single man who was unemployed at the time of his treatment. He lived on his own in an apartment and reported having a limited social life due to his wide-ranging social and performance concerns. During his initial assessment, Jeremy reported longstanding fears about the following situations: speaking to others, making small talk, starting conversations, maintaining eye contact, using the phone, and being in any situation where he felt he was the center of attention. As a result of the broad range of feared situations, criteria were met for SAD, generalized subtype.

Jeremy was taking paroxetine (20 mg per day) when he was seen at our clinic, and he continued to take this medication throughout the course of treatment. With his psychiatrist's cooperation, Jeremy agreed to maintain a stable dose of his medication throughout treatment to ensure that any positive changes in his symptoms could be attributed to his work in CBT.

Jeremy completed 20 sessions of individual CBT for his SAD. Similar to Susan's treatment, the first two sessions involved education about the treatment, identification of Jeremy's beliefs in social situations, instruction and practice in challenging these thoughts, identification of safety behaviors, and construction of an exposure hierarchy. Jeremy and his therapist identified his use of alcohol as a safety behavior. Jeremy reported using alcohol in social gatherings as a way of "loosening up" and feeling more relaxed. This included drinking excessively at family gatherings. Jeremy also avoided eye contact as a way to feel safer and protected, as though he might be less noticeable to others if he did not meet their gaze.

Jeremy's fears in these situations involved concerns that he would shake, stammer, or do something embarrassing for which others would then judge him negatively. He was also worried about having nothing to say or contribute, due to his current unemployment and limited social life. To examine and challenge some of these anxious thoughts, the therapist asked Jeremy about examples of times when these feared outcomes had come true. Jeremy was able to identify a number of times when he had been shaky in front of others, but had never received any negative feedback or insults about this. As a result, the therapist asked Jeremy to brainstorm all the possible things people could be thinking if they noticed him shaking. Jeremy was able to suggest that others might think that he was hungry or had a medical condition, in addition to thinking he had an anxiety problem. The therapist also asked Jeremy to consider for how long a person would think about his shaking if it was noticeable. When considering this question, Jeremy was able to see that such a major event to him (i.e., shaking) might not be so important to someone else, and that seeing someone who was shaking might not be all that interesting to a stranger. Further, Jeremy was asked to consider whether people really did notice his shaking when it happened. He had always assumed that others clearly noticed his shaking, but was open to testing this assumption out. He and the therapist decided to do an experiment in which the therapist modeled having shaky hands while doing several tasks (e.g., pushing a button on the elevator, paying for a coffee, and sipping coffee with a shaky hand). Jeremy shadowed the therapist as she modeled these behaviors, watching others' reactions and whether they looked at the therapist's hands. Much to his surprise, Jeremy observed that very few people even looked at the therapist while she was doing these tasks, and those who did appeared indifferent to her shaking hand. This experiment bolstered Jeremy's confidence in the idea that other people might not be so interested in what he is doing, even though he *feels* like he is the center of attention all the time.

When discussing Jeremy's fears of having nothing to say in conversations, his therapist asked him to think about what people talk about other than their work. Together, they brainstormed a number of other topics he could talk about with acquaintances (e.g., hobbies, pets, movies, books, news stories, etc.). By doing this exercise, the therapist implicitly challenged Jeremy's belief that one has to be employed to have something to say. Jeremy took it upon himself to do another experiment for homework, in which he listened to his mother talk on the phone to her friends. He reported back to his therapist that the topic of work rarely came up in his mother's conversations.

By the third session, the therapist introduced in-session exposures, based on Jeremy's exposure hierarchy (see Table 15).

Jeremy's initial exposures involved working on making eye contact with others. To demonstrate the importance of eye contact, the therapist asked Jeremy to report his reaction to her while she refused to make eye contact with him.

Jeremy: I don't like that. It makes me more nervous when you don't look at me.

Therapist: What about no eye contact makes you nervous?

Jeremy: It doesn't seem like you're interested in talking to me. It's like you just don't care or something.

Therapist: What do you make of that? How might your avoiding eye contact affect others?

Table 15
Jeremy's Exposure Hierarchy

Number	Item Description	Fear Rating (0–100)
1	Walking into a crowded room late.	100
2	Making hands shake on purpose while paying for something.	95
3	Telling a joke at a party.	95
4	Starting a conversation with an acquaintance.	90
5	Starting a conversation with a stranger.	80
6	Attending a family gathering without drinking alcohol.	70
7	Making small talk with a cashier or server.	65
8	Calling a friend on the phone.	60
9	Calling a store on the phone.	50
10	Asking strangers for the time or directions.	40
11	Making eye contact with the therapist.	40

Jeremy: Maybe people think I don't want to talk to them.

Therapist: That's possible. If you thought others didn't want to talk to you, how would that make you feel?

Jeremy: Crappy. Like I'm not important or interesting enough.

Therapist: What would you do in a situation like that?

Jeremy: Probably get away as fast as I could.

Therapist: Does this have any implications for situations you've been in?

Jeremy: Maybe I've scared people off by not looking at them in the eyes. Maybe they thought I didn't want to talk to them.

After Jeremy came to this realization about the possible negative impact of his limited use of eye contact, he was motivated to do exposures involving maintaining eye contact when talking to the therapist. Once he felt more comfortable with this, he agreed to be introduced to other staff members in the anxiety clinic where the therapist worked, with the goal of maintaining eye contact during the greeting. After numerous repetitions, Jeremy reported that his fear rating when maintaining eye contact had dropped to 20 out of 100. For homework, he practiced making eye contact with close friends and his parents.

Over the next several sessions, Jeremy tried in-session exposures involving asking others for the time, asking for directions, and making phone calls. He was able to continue in-session exposures for homework. For example, Jeremy set the goal of calling at least five stores each day to ask a basic question (e.g., hours of operation). He predicted that he would stammer when making the calls, not make sense in what he was asking, and that the person on the other end of the phone would get noticeably frustrated with him. After a week of this homework, Jeremy returned to his next session and reported that only one person had seemed frustrated with him, but this was a situation where he hadn't even messed up his question. Through cognitive restructuring, Jeremy decided it was more likely that this particular person was having a bad day or was a less friendly person than all the other people he talked to who were pleasant when answering his questions.

By Session 15, Jeremy was working on the more difficult items on his hierarchy. He ran into trouble, however, when trying to figure out how to make himself the center of attention. Originally, he and his therapist had decided that Jeremy would tell a joke at a party or enter a crowded room late as ways to make him feel like the center of attention. However, Jeremy didn't have a lot of opportunities to be at parties and he also could not think of where he could go to enter a crowded room. This problem required some creativity on Jeremy's and the therapist's part. Together, they found a weekly lecture series at a local university that was open to the public. Jeremy decided to attend the lectures, arriving just as the lecture was about to start so he would have pass people to find a seat. To further draw attention to himself, the therapist suggested that Jeremy purposely do things to his appearance to increase the likelihood of people noticing him. For example, Jeremy buttoned shirts incorrectly, wore winter hats on warm days, and purposely "forgot" something while grocery shopping, holding his line up while a clerk went to find him the missing item. These exposures allowed Jeremy to become more comfortable with being noticed by others, and allowed him to challenge his thoughts about how catastrophic this would be. Although Jeremy experienced a few "difficult" reactions from others (e.g., frustration from others in line at the grocery store), most people did not react to these scenarios, and Jeremy was surprised to realize how little people even looked at him while wearing his shirts buttoned incorrectly.

By the end of 20 sessions, Jeremy's anxiety symptoms were much reduced. He was attending family events on a regular basis and had joined a local gym where he had met a few new acquaintances. He reported increased confidence in himself and less concern about being "conspicuous" in public.

6

Further Reading

Readings for Professionals

Antony, M. M., Ledley, D. R., & Heimberg, R. G. (Eds.) (2005). *Improving outcomes and preventing relapse in cognitive behavioral therapy*. New York: Guilford.

Antony, M. M., & Swinson, R. P. (2000). *Phobic disorders and panic in adults: A guide to assessment and treatment*. Washington, DC: American Psychological Association.

Barlow, D. H. (Ed.) (2008). *Clinical handbook of psychological disorders, 4th edition*. New York: Guilford.

Crozier, W. R., & Alden, L. E. (Eds.) (2005). *The Essential Handbook of Social Anxiety for Clinicians*. Hoboken, NJ: Wiley.

Heimberg, R. G., & Becker, R. E. (2002). *Cognitive-behavioral group therapy for social phobia: Basic mechanisms and clinical strategies*. New York: Guilford.

Hofmann, S. G., & DiBartolo, P. M. (2001). *From social anxiety to social phobia: Multiple perspectives*. Needham Heights, MA: Allyn and Bacon.

Hope, D. A., Heimberg, R. G., & Turk, C. L. (2006). *Managing social anxiety: A cognitive behavioral therapy approach (therapist guide)*. New York: Oxford.

Kearney, C. A. (2005). *Social anxiety and social phobia in youth: Characteristics, assessment, and psychological treatment*. New York: Springer.

Readings for Consumers

Antony, M. M. (2004). *10 simple solutions to shyness: How to overcome shyness, social anxiety, and fear of public speaking*. Oakland, CA: New Harbinger.

Antony, M. M., & Swinson, R. P. (2008). *The shyness and social anxiety workbook: Proven, step-by-step techniques for overcoming your fear* (2nd ed.). Oakland, CA: New Harbinger.

Hope, D. A., Heimberg, R. G., Juster, H. R., & Turk, C. L. (2000). *Managing social anxiety*. New York: Oxford.

Kase, L., & Monarth, H. (2007). *The confident speaker: Beat your nerves and communicate at your best in any situation*. New York: McGraw-Hill.

Stein, M. B., & Walker, J. R. (2001). *Triumph over shyness: Conquering shyness and social anxiety*. New York: McGraw Hill.

Video Resources

Albano, A. M. (2006). *Shyness and social phobia* (DVD). Washington, DC: American Psychological Association.

Rapee, R. M. (1999). *I think they think...Overcoming social phobia* (DVD or VHS Video). New York: Guilford.

7

References

Albano, A. M., & Detweiler, M. F. (2001). The developmental and clinical impact of social anxiety and social phobia in children and adolescents. In S. G. Hofmann, & P. M. DiBartolo (Eds.), *From social anxiety to social phobia* (pp. 162–178). Boston, MA: Allyn & Bacon.

Albano, A. M., & DiBartolo, P. M. (2007). *Cognitive-behavioral therapy for social phobia in adolescents: Stand up, speak out.* New York: Oxford.

Al-Kubaisy, T., Marks, I. M., Logsdail, S., Marks, M. P., Lovell, K., Sungur, M., & Araya, R. (1992). Role of exposure homework in phobia reduction: A controlled study. *Behavior Therapy, 23,* 599–621.

American Psychiatric Association. (2000). *Diagnostic and statistical manual of mental disorders* (4th ed., text revision). Washington, DC: Author.

Antony, M. M. (2004). *10 simple solutions to shyness: How to overcome shyness, social anxiety, and fear of public speaking.* Oakland, CA: New Harbinger Publications.

Antony, M. M., Coons, M. J., McCabe, R. E., Ashbaugh, A. R., & Swinson, R. P. (2006). Psychometric properties of the Social Phobia Inventory: Further evaluation. *Behaviour Research and Therapy, 44,* 1177–1185.

Antony, M. M., Ledley, D. R., Liss, A., & Swinson, R.P. (2006). Responses to symptom induction exercises in panic disorder. *Behaviour Research and Therapy, 44,* 85–98.

Antony, M. M., & McCabe, R. E. (2004). *10 simple solutions to panic: How to overcome panic attacks, calm physical symptoms, and reclaim your life.* Oakland, CA: New Harbinger Publications.

Antony, M. M., Orsillo, S. M., & Roemer, L. (2001). *Practitioner's guide to empirically based measures of anxiety.* New York: Springer.

Antony, M. M., & Roemer, L. (2003). Behavior therapy. In A. S. Gurman and S. B. Messer (Eds.), *Essential psychotherapies: Theory and practice* (2nd ed., pp. 182–223). New York: Guilford.

Antony, M. M., Roth, D., Swinson, R. P., Huta, V., & Devins, G.M. (1998). Illness intrusiveness in individuals with panic disorder, obsessive-compulsive disorder, or social phobia. *Journal of Nervous and Mental Disease, 186,* 311–315.

Antony, M. M., & Swinson, R. P. (2000). *Phobic disorders and panic in adults: A guide to assessment and treatment.* Washington, DC: American Psychological Association.

Antony, M. M., & Swinson, R. P. (2008). *The shyness and social anxiety workbook: Proven, step-by-step techniques for overcoming your fear* (2nd ed.). Oakland, CA: New Harbinger Publications.

Arkowitz, H., Westra, H. A., Miller, W. R., & Rollnick, S. (2008). *Motivational interviewing in the treatment of psychological problems.* New York: Guilford.

Asmal, L., & Stein, D. J. (in press). Anxiety and culture. In M. M. Antony & M. B. Stein (Eds.), *Oxford handbook of anxiety and related disorders.* New York: Oxford.

Ayers, C. R., Thorp, S. R., & Wetherell, J. L. (in press). Anxiety disorders and hoarding in older adults. In M. M. Antony & M. B. Stein (Eds.), *Oxford handbook of anxiety and related disorders.* New York: Oxford.

Barlow, D. H. (Ed.) (2008). *Clinical handbook of psychological disorders* (4th ed.). New York: Guilford.

Beck, A. T., Emery, G., & Greenberg, R. (1985). *Anxiety disorders and phobias: A cognitive perspective.* New York: Basic Books.

Bernstein, D. A., Borkovec, T. D., & Hazlett-Stevens, H. (2000). *New directions in progressive relaxation training: A guidebook for helping professionals.* Westport, CT: Praeger.

Bieling, P. J., McCabe, R. E., & Antony, M. M. (2006). *Cognitive behavioral therapy in groups.* New York: Guilford.

Blomhoff, S., Haug, T. T., Hellström, K., Holme, I., Humble, M., Madsbu, H. P., & Wold, J. E. (2001). Randomised controlled general practice trial of sertraline, exposure therapy and combined treatment in generalised social phobia. *British Journal of Psychiatry, 179,* 23–30.

Blöte, A., & Westenberg, P. M. (2007). Socially anxious adolescents' perception of treatment by classmates. *Behaviour Research and Therapy, 45,* 189–198.

Bögels, S. M., & Reith, W. (1999). Validity of two questionnaires to assess social fears: The Dutch Social Phobia and Anxiety Inventory and the Blushing, Trembling, and Sweating Questionnaire. *Journal of Psychopathology and Behavioral Assessment, 21,* 51–66.

Bögels, S. M., van Oosten, A., Muris, P., & Smulders, D. (2001). Familial correlates of social anxiety in children and adolescents. *Behaviour Research and Therapy, 39,* 273–287.

Brown, E. J., Heimberg, R. G., & Juster, H. R. (1995). Social phobia subtype and avoidant personality disorder: Effect on severity of social phobia, impairment, and outcome of cognitive-behavioral treatment. *Behavior Therapy, 26,* 467–486.

Brown, T. A., Campbell, L. A., Lehman, C. L., Grisham, J. R., & Mancill, R. B. (2001). Current and lifetime comorbidity of the DSM-IV anxiety and mood disorders in a large clinical sample. *Journal of Abnormal Psychology, 110,* 585–599.

Brown, T. A., Di Nardo, P. A., Lehman, C. L., & Campbell, L. A. (2001). Reliability of DSM-IV anxiety and mood disorders: Implications for the classification of emotional disorders. *Journal of Abnormal Psychology, 110,* 49–58.

Cairney, J., McCabe, L., Veldhuizen, S., Corna, L. M., Streiner, D., & Herrmann, N. (2007). Epidemiology of social phobia in later life. *American Journal of Geriatric Psychiatry, 15,* 224–233.

Chambless, D. L., & Hope, D. A. (1996). Cognitive approaches to the psychopathology and treatment of social phobia. In P. M. Salkovskis (Ed.), *Frontiers of cognitive therapy* (pp. 345–382). New York: Guilford.

Chambless, D. L., Tran, G. Q., & Glass, C. R. (1997). Predictors of response to cognitive-behavioral group therapy for social phobia. *Journal of Anxiety Disorders, 11,* 221–240.

Chartier, M. J., Walker, J. R., & Stein, M. B. (2003). Considering comorbidity in social phobia. *Social Psychiatry and Psychiatric Epidemiology, 38,* 728–734.

Cho, Y., Smits, J. A. J., & Telch, M. J. (2004). The Speech Anxiety Thoughts Inventory: Scale development and preliminary psychometric data. *Behaviour Research and Therapy, 42,* 13–25.

Chorpita, B. F. (2007). *Modular cognitive-behavioral therapy for childhood anxiety disorders.* New York: Guilford.

Clark, D. M., Ehlers, A., Hackmann, A., McManus, F., Fennell, M., Grey, N., Waddington, L., & Wild, J. (2006). Cognitive therapy versus exposure and applied relaxation in social phobia: A randomized controlled trial. *Journal of Consulting and Clinical Psychology, 74,* 568–578.

Clark, D. M., Ehlers, A., McManus, F., Hackmann, A., Fennell, M., Campbell, H., et al. (2003). Cognitive therapy vs. fluoxetine in generalized social phobia: A randomized placebo controlled trial. *Journal of Consulting and Clinical Psychology, 71,* 1058–1067.

Clark, D. M., & Wells, A. (1995). A cognitive model of social phobia. In R. G. Heimberg, M. R. Liebowitz, D. A. Hope, & F. R. Schneier. (Eds). *Social phobia: Diagnosis, assessment, and treatment* (pp. 69–93). New York: Guilford.

Cohen, J. (1988). *Statistical power analysis for the behavioral sciences* (2nd ed.). Hillsdale, NJ: Lawrence Erlbaum Associates.

Connor, K. M., Davidson, J. R. T., Churchill, L. E., Sherwood, A., Weisler, R. H., & Foa, E. (2000). Psychometric properties of the Social Phobia Inventory (SPIN). *British Journal of Psychiatry, 176,* 379–386.

Craske, M. G., & Mystkowski, J. L. (2006). Exposure therapy and extinction: Clinical studies. In M. G. Craske, D. Hermans, & D. Vansteenwegen (Eds.), *Fear and learn-*

ing: From basic processes to clinical implications (pp. 217–233). Washington, DC: American Psychological Association.

Dadds, M., Barrett, P., Rapee, R., & Ryan, S. (1996). Family process and child anxiety and aggression: An observational analysis. *Journal of Abnormal Child Psychology, 24,* 715–734.

Davidson, J. R., Foa, E. B., Huppert, J. D., Keefe, F. J., Franklin, M. E., Compton, J. S., et al. (2004). Fluoxetine, comprehensive cognitive behavioral therapy, and placebo in generalized social phobia. *Archives of General Psychiatry, 61,* 1005–1013.

Davidson, J. R. T., Miner, C. M., De Veaugh-Geiss, J., Tupler, L. A., Colket, J. T., & Potts, N. L. S. (1997). The Brief Social Phobia Scale: A psychometric evaluation. *Psychological Medicine, 27,* 161–166.

Davidson, J. R. T., Potts, N. L. S., Richichi, E. A., Ford, S. M., Krishnan, R. R., Smith, R. D., & Wilson, W. (1991). The Brief Social Phobia Scale. *Journal of Clinical Psychiatry, 52,* 48–51.

Deacon, B., & Abramowitz, J. (2006). Anxiety sensitivity and its dimensions across the anxiety disorders. *Journal of Anxiety Disorders, 20,* 837–857.

Devins, G. M., Binik, Y. M., Hutchinson, T. A., Hollomby, D. J., Barre, P. E., & Guttman, R. D. (1983). The emotional impact of end-stage renal disease: Importance of patient's perceptions of intrusiveness and control. *International Journal of Psychiatry and Medicine, 13,* 327–343.

Di Nardo, P. A., Brown, T. A., & Barlow, D. H. (1994). *Anxiety Disorders Interview Schedule for DSM-IV: Lifetime version* (ADIS-IV-L). New York: Oxford.

Eaton, W. W., Dryman, A., & Weissman, M. M. (1991). Panic and phobia. In L. N. Robins & D. A. Regier (Eds.), *Psychiatric disorders in America: The Epidemiological Catchment Area Study* (pp. 155–179). New York: The Free Press.

Edelman, R. E., & Chambless, D. L. (1995). Adherence during sessions and homework in cognitive-behavioral group treatment of social phobia. *Behaviour Research and Therapy, 33,* 573–577.

Erwin, B. A., Heimberg, R. G., Juster, H., & Mindlin, M. (2002). Comorbid anxiety and mood disorders among persons with social anxiety disorder. *Behaviour Research and Therapy, 40,* 19–35.

Erwin, B. A., Heimberg, R. G., Schneier, F. R., & Liebowitz, M. R. (2003). Anger experience and anger expression in social anxiety disorder: Pretreatment profile and predictors of attrition and response to cognitive-behavioral treatment. *Behavior Therapy, 34,* 331–350.

Federoff, I. C., & Taylor, S. (2001). Psychological and pharmacological treatments of social phobia: A meta-analysis. *Journal of Clinical Pharmacology, 21,* 311–324.

Fehm, L., Pelissolo, A., Furmark, T., & Wittchen, H. (2005). Size and burden of social phobia in Europe. *European Neuropsychopharmacology, 15,* 453–462.

Ferrell, C. B., Beidel, D. C., & Turner, S. M. (2004). Assessment and treatment of socially phobic children: A cross-cultural comparison. *Journal of Clinical Child and Adolescent Psychology, 33,* 260–268.

Feske, U., & Chambless, D. L. (1995). Cognitive behavioral versus exposure only treatment for social phobia: A meta-analysis. *Behavior Therapy, 26,* 695–720.

First, M. B., Spitzer, R. L., Gibbon, M., & Williams, J. B. W. (1996). *Structured Clinical Interview for DSM-IV Axis I Disorders – Patient Edition* (SCID-I/P, Version 2.0). New York: Biometrics Research Department, New York State Psychiatric Institute.

Foa, E. B., Jameson, J. S., Turner, R. M., & Payne, L. L. (1980). Massed vs. spaced exposure sessions in the treatment of agoraphobia. *Behaviour Research and Therapy, 18,* 333–338.

Foa, E. B., & Kozak, M. J. (1986). Emotional processing of fear: Exposure to corrective information. *Psychological Bulletin, 99,* 20–35.

Furr, J. M., Tiwari, S., Suveg, C., & Kendall, P. C. (in press). Anxiety disorders in children and adolescents. In M. M. Antony & M. B. Stein (Eds.), *Oxford handbook of anxiety and related disorders.* New York: Oxford.

Fydrich, T., Chambless, D. L., Perry, K.J., Buergener, F., & Beazley, M. B. (1998). Behavioral assessment of social performance: A rating system for social phobia. *Behaviour Research and Therapy, 36,* 995–1010.

Garcia-Palacios, A., & Botella, C. (2003). The effects of dropping in-situation safety behaviors in the treatment of social phobia. *Behavioral interventions, 18,* 23–33.

Gerlenter, C. S., Uhde, T. W., Cimbolic, P., Arnkoff, D. B., Vittone, B. J., Tancer, M. E., & Bartko, J. J. (1991). Cognitive-behavioral and pharmacological treatments of social phobia: A controlled study. *Archives of General Psychiatry, 48,* 938–945.

Gifford, S., Purdon, C., Rowa, K., Young, L. & Antony, M. M. (2005, November). *Treatment fears in obsessive-compulsive disorder, panic disorder/agoraphobia, and social phobia.* Paper presented at the meeting of the Association for Behavioral and Cognitive Therapies, Washington, DC.

Gladstone, G. L., Parker, G. B., & Malhi, G. S. (2006). Do bullied children become anxious and depressed adults? A cross-sectional investigation of the correlates of bullying and anxious depression. *Journal of Nervous and Mental Disease, 194,* 201–208.

Gould, R. A., Buckminster, S., Pollack, M. H., Otto, M. W., & Yap, L. (1997). Cognitive-behavioral and pharmacological treatment for social phobia: A meta-analysis. *Clinical Psychology: Science and Practice, 4,* 291–306.

Greenberger, D., & Padesky, C. A. (1995). *Mind over mood: Change the way you feel by changing the way you think.* New York: Guilford.

Haug, T. T., Blomhoff, S., Hellstrøm, K., Holme, I., Humble, M., Madsbu, H. P., & Wold, J. E. (2003). Exposure therapy and sertraline in social phobia: 1-year follow-up of a randomised controlled trial. *British Journal of Psychiatry, 182,* 312–318.

Heimberg, R. G. (2002). Cognitive behavioral therapy for social anxiety disorder: Current status and future directions. *Biological Psychiatry, 51,* 101–108.

Heimberg, R. G., & Becker, R. E. (2002). *Cognitive-behavioral group therapy for social phobia: Basic mechanisms and clinical strategies.* New York: Guilford.

Heimberg, R. G., Dodge, C. S., Hope, D. A., Kennedy, C. R., Zollo, L., & Becker, R.E. (1990). Cognitive-behavioral group treatment of social phobia: Comparison to a credible placebo control. *Cognitive Therapy and Research, 14,* 1–23.

Heimberg, R. G., Horner, K. J., Juster, H. R., Safren, S. A., Brown, E. J., Schneier, F. R., & Liebowitz, M. R. (1999). Psychometric properties of the Liebowitz Social Anxiety Scale. *Psychological Medicine, 29,* 199–212.

Heimberg, R. G., Liebowitz, M. R., Hope, D. A., Schneier, F. R., Holt, C. S., Welkowitz, L., et al. (1998). Cognitive-behavioral group therapy versus phenelzine in social phobia: 12 week outcome. *Archives of General Psychiatry, 55,* 1133–1141.

Heimberg, R. G., Makris, G. S., Juster, H. R., Öst, L.-G., & Rapee, R. M. (1997). Social phobia: A preliminary cross-national comparison. *Depression and Anxiety, 5,* 130–133.

Heimberg, R. G., Salzman, D. G., Holt, C. S., & Blendell, K. A. (1993). Cognitive-behavioral group treatment for social phobia: Effectiveness at five-year follow-up. *Cognitive Therapy and Research, 17,* 325–339.

Henderson, L., & Zimbardo, P. (1998). Shyness. In H.S. Friedman (Ed.), *Encyclopedia of mental health* (vol. 3, pp. 497–509). San Diego, CA: Academic Press.

Herbert, J. D., Gaudiano, B. A., Rheingold, A. A., Myers, V. H., Dalrymple, K., & Nolan, E. M. (2005). Social skills training augments the effectiveness of cognitive behavioral group therapy for social anxiety disorder. *Behavior Therapy, 36,* 125–138.

Herbert, J. D., Rheingold, A. A., Gaudiano, B. A., & Myers, V. H. (2004). Standard versus extended cognitive behavior therapy for social anxiety disorder: A randomized-controlled trial. *Behavioural and Cognitive Psychotherapy, 32,* 131–147.

Hettema, J. M., Prescott, C. A., Myers, J. M., Neale, M. C., & Kendler, K. M. (2005). The structure of genetic and environmental risk factors for anxiety disorders in men and women. *Archives of General Psychiatry, 62,* 182–189.

Hirshfeld-Becker, D. R., Biederman, J., Caltharp, S., Rosenbaum, E. D., Faraone, S. V., & Rosenbaum, J. F. (2003). Behavioral inhibition and disinhibition as hypothesized precursors to psychopathology: Implications for pediatric bipolar disorder. *Biological Psychiatry, 53,* 985–999.

Hofmann, S. G., & Barlow, D. H. (2002). Social phobia (social anxiety disorder). In D. H. Barlow (Ed.), *Anxiety and its disorders: The nature and treatment of anxiety and panic* (2nd ed., pp. 454–476). New York: Guilford.

Hofmann, S. G., Meuret, A. E., Smits, J. A. J., Simon, N. M., Pollack, M. H., Eisenmenger, K., et al. (2006). Augmentation of exposure therapy with D-cycloserine for social anxiety disorder. *Archives of General Psychiatry, 63,* 298–304.

Hope, D. A., Heimberg, R .G., & Bruch, M. A. (1995). Dismantling cognitive-behavioral group therapy for social phobia. *Behaviour Research and Therapy, 33,* 637–650.

Hope, D. A., Heimberg, R. G., & Turk, C. L. (2006). *Managing social anxiety: A cognitive behavioral therapy approach (therapist guide).* New York: Oxford.

Hudson, J. L., & Rapee, R. M. (2001). Parent-child interactions and anxiety disorders: An observational study. *Behaviour Research and Therapy, 39,* 1411–1427.

Hwu, H. G., Yeh, E. K., & Chang, L. Y. (1989). Prevalence of psychiatric disorders in Taiwan defined by the Chinese Diagnostic Interview Schedule. *Acta Psychiatrica Scandinavica, 79,* 136–147.

Jerremalm, A., Jansson, L., & Öst, L.-G. (1986). Cognitive and physiological reactivity and the effects of different behavioral methods in the treatment of social phobia. *Behaviour Research and Therapy, 24,* 171–180.

Jerremalm, A., Johansson, J., & Öst, L.-G. (1980). Applied relaxation as a self-control technique for social phobia. *Scandinavian Journal of Behavioral Therapy, 9,* 35–43.

Kearney, C. A. (2005). *Social anxiety and social phobia in youth: Characteristics, assessment, and psychological treatment.* New York: Springer.

Keller, M. B. (2003). The lifelong course of social anxiety disorder: A clinical perspective. *Acta Psychiatrica Scandinavica, 108,* 85–94.

Kendall, P. C., Flannery-Schroeder, E., Panichelli-Mindel, S. M., Southam-Gerow, M., Henin, A., & Warman, M. (1997). Therapy for youths with anxiety disorders: A second randomized clinical trial. *Journal of Consulting and Clinical Psychology, 65,* 366–380.

Kendler, K. S., Neale, M. C., Kessler, R. C., Heath, A. C., & Eaves, L. J. (1992). The genetic epidemiology of phobias in women: The interrelationship of agoraphobia, social phobia, situational phobia, and simple phobia, *Archives of General Psychiatry, 49,* 273–281.

Kessler, R. C., Berglund, P., Demler, O., Jin, R., Merikangas, K. R., & Walters, E. E. (2005). Lifetime prevalence and age-of-onset distributions of DSM-IV disorders in the National Comorbidity Survey Replication. *Archives of General Psychiatry, 62,* 593–602.

Kessler, R. C., McGonagle, K. A., Zhao, S., Nelson, C. B, Hughes, M., Eshleman, S., et al. (1994). Lifetime and 12-month prevalence of DSM-III-R psychiatric disorders in the United States: Results from the National Comorbidity Survey. *Archives of General Psychiatry, 51,* 8–19.

Kim, E.-J. (2005). The effect of the decreased safety behaviors on anxiety and negative thoughts in social phobics. *Journal of Anxiety Disorders, 19,* 69–86.

Kirmayer, L. J. (1991). The place of culture in psychiatric nosology: Taijin Kyofusho and DSM-III-R. *The Journal of Nervous and Mental Disease, 179,* 19–28.

Klonsky, B. G., Dutton, D. L., & Liebel, C. N. (1990). Developmental antecedents of private self-consciousness, public self-consciousness, and social anxiety. *Genetic, Social, and General Psychology Monographs, 116,* 275–297.

Ledley, D. A., & Heimberg, R. G. (2005). Social anxiety disorder. In M. M. Antony, D. R. Ledley, & R. G. Heimberg (Eds.) (2005). *Improving outcomes and preventing relapse in cognitive behavioral therapy.* New York: Guilford.

Leung, A. W., & Heimberg, R. G. (1996). Homework compliance, perceptions of control, and outcome of cognitive-behavioral treatment of social phobia. *Behaviour Research and Therapy, 34,* 423–432.

Levin, A. P., Saoud, J .B., Strauman, T., Gorman, J. M., Fyer, A., Crawford, R., & Liebowitz, M. R. (1993). Responses of "generalized" and "discrete" social phobics during public speaking. *Journal of Anxiety Disorders, 7,* 207–221.

Liebowitz, M. R. (1987). Social Phobia. *Modern Problems of Pharmacopsychiatry, 22,* 141–173.

Liebowitz, M. R., Heimberg, R. G., Schneier, F. R., Hope, D. A., Davies, S., Holt, C. S., et al. (1999). Cognitive-behavioral group therapy versus phenelzine in social phobia: Long term outcome. *Depression and Anxiety, 10,* 89–98.

Lucas, R. A., & Telch, M. J. (1993, November). *Group versus individual treatment of social phobia*. Paper presented at the meeting of the Association for Advancement of Behavior Therapy, Atlanta, GA.

Magee, L., Erwin, B. A., & Heimberg, R. G. (in press). Psychological treatment for social anxiety disorder and specific phobia. In M. M. Antony & M. B. Stein (Eds.), *Oxford handbook of anxiety and related disorders*. New York: Oxford.

Marks, I. M., Swinson, R. P., Başoğlu, M., Kuch, K., Noshirvani, H., O'Sullivan, G., et al. (1993). Alprazolam and exposure alone and combined in panic disorder with agoraphobia: A controlled study in London and Toronto. *British Journal of Psychiatry, 162,* 776–787.

Massion, A. O., Dyck, I. R., Shea, M. T., Phillips, K. A., Warshaw, M. G., & Keller, M. B. (2002). Personality disorders and time to remission in generalized anxiety disorders, social phobia, and panic disorder. *Archives of General Psychiatry, 59,* 434–440.

Mattick, R. P., & Clarke, J. C. (1998). Development and validation of measures of social phobia scrutiny fear and social interaction anxiety. *Behaviour Research and Therapy, 36,* 455–470.

Mattick, R. P., & Peters, L. (1988). Treatment of severe social phobia: Effects of guided exposure with and without cognitive restructuring. *Journal of Consulting and Clinical Psychology, 56,* 251–260.

Mattick, R. P., Peters, L., & Clarke, J. C. (1989). Exposure and cognitive restructuring for social phobia: A controlled study. *Behavior Therapy, 20,* 3–23.

McCabe, R. E., Antony, M. M., Summerfeldt, L. J., Liss, A., & Swinson, R. P. (2003). Preliminary examination of the relationship between anxiety disorders in adults and self-reported history of teasing or bullying experiences. *Cognitive Behaviour Therapy, 32,* 187–193.

McHolm, A. E., Cunningham, C. E., & Vanier, M. K. (2005). *Helping your child with selective mutism: Practical steps to overcome a fear of speaking.* Oakland, CA: New Harbinger.

McKay, M., Davis, M., & Fanning, P. (1995). *Messages: The communications skills book* (2nd ed.). Oakland, CA: New Harbinger.

Mennin, D. S., Heimberg, R. G., & MacAndrew, S. J. (2000). Comorbid generalized anxiety disorder in primary social phobia: Symptom severity, functional impairment, and treatment response. *Journal of Anxiety Disorders, 14,* 325–343.

Mersch, P. P. (1995). The treatment of social phobia: The differential effectiveness of exposure in vivo and an integration of exposure in vivo, rational emotive therapy and social skills training. *Behaviour Research and Therapy, 33,* 259–269.

Miller, W. R., & Rollnick, S. (2002). *Motivational interviewing: Preparing people for change* (2nd ed.). New York: Guilford.

Mineka, S., & Thomas, C. (1999). Mechanisms of change in exposure therapy for anxiety disorders. In T. Dalgleish & M. J. Power (Eds.), *Cognition and emotion* (pp. 747–764). New York: Wiley.

Mohlman, J., Gorenstein, E. E., Kleber, M., de Jesus, M., Gorman, J. M., & Papp, L. A. (2003). Standard and enhanced cognitive-behavior therapy for late-life generalized anxiety disorder: Two pilot investigations. *American Journal of Geriatric Psychiatry, 11,* 24–32.

Morgan, H., & Raffle, C. (1999). Does reducing safety behaviors improve treatment response in patients with social phobia? *Australian and New Zealand Journal of Psychiatry, 33,* 503–510.

Mörtberg, E., Clark, D. M., Sundin, Ö., Åberg, W. A., & Wistedt, A. (2007). Intensive group cognitive treatment and individual cognitive therapy vs. treatment as usual in social phobia: A randomized controlled trial. *Acta Psychiatrica Scandinavica, 115,* 142–154.

Moscovitch, D. A., Antony, M.M., & Swinson, R. P. (in press). Exposure-based treatments for anxiety disorders: Theory and process. In M. M. Antony & M. B. Stein (Eds.), *Oxford handbook of anxiety and related disorders*. New York: Oxford.

Mulkens, S., de Jong, P. J., Dobbelaar, A., & Bögels, S. M. (1999). Fear of blushing: Fearful preoccupation irrespective of facial coloration. *Behaviour Research and Therapy, 37,* 1119–1128.

Neal J., & Edelmann R. J. (2003). The etiology of social phobia: Toward a developmental profile. *Clinical Psychology Review, 23,* 761–86.

Newman, M. G., Hofmann, S. G., Trabert, W., Roth, W. T., & Taylor, S. (1994). Does behavioral treatment of social phobia lead to cognitive changes? *Behavior Therapy, 25,* 503–517.

Norton, P. J. (in press). Integrated psychological treatment of multiple anxiety disorders. In M. M. Antony & M. B. Stein (Eds.), *Oxford handbook of anxiety and related disorders.* New York: Oxford.

Oosterbaan, D. B., van Balkom, A. J. L. M., Spinoven, P., van Oppen, P., & van Dyck, R. (2001). Cognitive therapy versus moclobemide in social phobia: A controlled study. *Clinical Psychology and Psychotherapy, 8,* 263–273.

Orsillo, S. M. (2001). Measure for social phobia. In M. M. Antony, S. M. Orsillo, & L. Roemer (Eds.), *Practitioner's guide to empirically based measures of anxiety* (pp. 165–187). New York: Springer.

Osberg, J. W. (1981). The effectiveness of applied relaxation in the treatment of speech anxiety. *Behavior Therapy, 12,* 723–729.

Öst, L.-G., & Hugdahl., K. (1981). Acquisition of phobias and anxiety response patterns in clinical patients. *Behaviour Research and Therapy, 19,* 439–447.

Öst, L., Sedvall, H., Breitholz, E., Hellström, K., & Lindwall, R. (1995, July). *Cognitive-behavioral treatment for social phobia: Individual, group, and self-administered treatment.* Paper presented at the meeting of the World Congress of Behavioural and Cognitive Therapies, Copenhagen, Denmark.

Otto, M. W., Pollack, M. H., Gould, R. A., Worthington, J. J., McArdle, E. T., Rosenbaum, J. F., & Heimberg, R. G. (2000). A comparison of the efficacy of clonazepam and cognitive-behavioral group therapy for the treatment of social phobia. *Journal of Anxiety Disorders, 14,* 345–358.

Peterson, R. A., & Reiss, S. (1993). *Anxiety Sensitivity Index Revised Test Manual.* Worthington, OH: IDS Publishing Corporation.

Pina, A. A., Silverman, W. K., Fuentes, R. M., Kurtines, W. M., & Weems, C. F. (2003). Exposure-based cognitive-behavioral treatment for phobic and anxiety disorders: treatment effects and maintenance for Hispanic/Latino relative to European-American youths. *Journal of the American Academy of Child and Adolescent Psychiatry, 42,* 1179–1187.

Pinto-Gouveia, J., Cunha, M. I., do Céo Salvador, M. (2003). Assessment of social phobia by self-report questionnaires: The Social Interaction and Performance Anxiety and Avoidance Scale and the Social Phobia Safety Behaviours Scale. *Behavioural and Cognitive Psychotherapy, 31,* 291–311.

Prasko, J., Dockery, C., Horacek, J., Houbova, P., Kosova, J., Klaschka, J., et al. (2006). Moclobemide and cognitive behavioral therapy in the treatment of social phobia. A six-month controlled study and 24 months follow up. *Neuroendocrinology Letters, 27,* 473–481.

Purdon, C., Antony, M. M., Monteiro, S., & Swinson, R.P. (2001). Social anxiety in college students. *Journal of Anxiety Disorders, 15,* 203–215.

Rachman, S. (1977). The conditioning theory of fear-acquisition: A critical examination. *Behaviour Research and Therapy, 15,* 375–387.

Rachman, S. J. (1996). Mechanisms of action of cognitive-behavior treatment of anxiety disorders. In M. R. Mavissakalian & R. F. Prien (Eds.), *Long term treatments of anxiety disorders.* Washington DC: American Psychiatric Press

Rapee, R. M., & Heimberg, R. G. (1997). A cognitive-behavioural model of anxiety in social phobia. *Behaviour Research and Therapy, 35,* 741–756.

Rapee, R. M., & Lim, L. (1992). *Discrepancy* between self- and observer ratings of performance in social phobics. *Journal of Abnormal Psychology, 101,* 728–731.

Rapee, R. M., Spence, S. H., Cobham, V., & Wignall, A. (2000). *Helping your anxious child: A step-by-step guide for parents.* Oakland, CA: New Harbinger.

Rapee, R. M., Wignall, A., Hudson, J. L., & Schniering, C. A. (2000). *Treating anxious children and adolescents: An evidence-based approach.* Oakland, CA: New Harbinger.

Reich, J., Goldenberg, I., Vasile, R., Goisman, R., & Keller, M. (1994). A prospective follow-along study of the course of social phobia. *Psychiatry Research, 54,* 249–258.

Rescorla, R. A. (2001). Experimental extinction. In R. R. Mowrer & S. B. Klein (Eds.) *Handbook of contemporary learning theories* (pp. 119–154). Mahwah, NJ: Erlbaum.

Rodebaugh, T. L., Heimberg, R. G., Woods, C. M., Liebowitz, M. R., & Schneier, F. R. (2006). The factor structure and screening utility of the social interaction anxiety scale. *Psychological Assessment, 18,* 231–237.

Rodebaugh, T. L., Holaway, R. M., & Heimberg, R. G. (2004). The treatment of social anxiety disorder. *Clinical Psychology Review, 24,* 883–908.

Rosser, S., Erskine, A., & Crino, R. (2004). Pre-existing antidepressants and the outcome of group cognitive behaviour therapy for social phobia. *Australian and New Zealand Journal of Psychiatry, 38,* 233–239.

Roth, D., Coles, M., & Heimberg, R. G. (2002). The relationship between memories for childhood teasing and anxiety and depression in adulthood. *Journal of Anxiety Disorders, 16,* 151–166.

Rowa, K., & Antony, M. M. (in press). Generalized anxiety disorder. In W. E. Craighead, D. J. Miklowitz, & L. W. Craighead (Eds.), *Psychopathology.* Hoboken, NJ: Wiley.

Rubin, K. H., & Mills, R. S. L. (1988). The many faces of social isolation in childhood. *Journal of Consulting and Clinical Psychology, 56,* 916–924.

Safran, J. D. & Segal, Z. V. (1996). *Interpersonal process in cognitive therapy.* Lanham, MD: Jason Aronson.

Safren, S. A., Heimberg, R. G., & Juster, H. R. (1997). Client expectancies and their relationship to pretreatment symtomatology and outcome of cognitive-behavioral group treatment for social phobia. *Journal of Consulting and Clinical Psychology, 65,* 694–698.

Scholing, A., & Emmelkamp, P. M. (1993). Exposure with and without cognitive therapy for generalized social phobia: Effects of individual and group treatment. *Behaviour Research and Therapy, 31,* 667–681.

Schuurmans, J., Comijs, H., Emmelkamp, P. M., Gundy, C. M., Weijnen, I., van den Hout, M., & van Dyck, R. (2006). A randomized, controlled trial of the effectiveness of cognitive-behavioral therapy and sertraline versus a waitlist control group for anxiety disorders in older adults. *American Journal of Geriatric Psychiatry, 14,* 255–263.

Simpson, H. B., Schneier, F. R., Campeas, R. B., Marshall, R. D., Fallon, B .A., Davies, S., et al. (1998). Imipramine in the treatment of social phobia. *Journal of Clinical Psychopharmacology, 18,* 132–135.

Somers, J. M., Goldner, E. M., Waraich, P., & Hsu, L. (2006). Prevalence and incidence studies of anxiety disorders: A systematic review of the literature. *Canadian Journal of Psychiatry, 51,* 100–113.

Spence, S. H., Donovan, C., & Brechman-Toussaint, M. (1999). Social skills, social outcomes, and cognitive features of childhood social phobia. *Journal of Abnormal Psychology, 108,* 211–221.

Stangier, U., Heidenreich, T., & Schermelleh-Engel, K. (2006). Safety behaviors and social performance in patients with generalized social phobia. *Journal of Cognitive Psychotherapy, 20,* 17–31.

Stangier, U., Heidenreich, T., Peitz, M., Lauterbach, W., & Clark, D. M. (2003). Cognitive therapy for social phobia: Individual versus group treatment. *Behaviour Research and Therapy, 41,* 991–1007.

Stein, M. B., Fuetsch, M., Müller, N., Höfler, M., Lieb, R., & Wittchen, H.-U. (2001). Social anxiety disorder and the risk of depression: A prospective community study of adolescents and young adults. *Archives of General Psychiatry, 58,* 251–256.

Stein, M. B., Jang, K. L., & Livesley, W. J. (2002). Heritability of social anxiety-related concerns and personality characteristics: A twin study. *Journal of Nervous and Mental Disease, 190,* 219–224.

Strunk, D. R., Huppert, J. D., Foa, E. B., & Davidson, J. R. T. (2003, November). Generalized social phobia and avoidant personality disorder: Defining and distinguishing constructs. Paper presented at the meeting of the Association for Advancement of Behavior Therapy, Boston, MA.

Swinson, R. P., Antony, M. M., Bleau, P., Chokka, P., Craven, M., Fallu, A., et al. (2006). Clinical practice guidelines: Management of anxiety disorders. *Canadian Journal of Psychiatry, 51* (Suppl. 2), 1S–92S.

Taube-Schiff, M., Suvak, M. K., Antony, M. M., Bieling, P. J., & McCabe, R. E. (2007). Group cohesion in cognitive behavioral group therapy for social phobia. *Behaviour Research and Therapy, 45,* 687–698.

Taylor, S. (1996). Meta-analysis of cognitive-behavioral treatments for social phobia. *Journal of Behavior Therapy and Experimental Psychiatry, 27,* 1–9.

Taylor, S., & Cox, B. J. (1998). An expanded Anxiety Sensitivity Index: Evidence for a hierarchic structure in a clinical sample. *Journal of Anxiety Disorders, 12,* 463–483.

Taylor, S., Koch, W. J., & McNally, R. J. (1992). How does anxiety sensitivity vary across the anxiety disorders? *Journal of Anxiety Disorders, 6,* 249–259.

Taylor, S., Zvolendky, M. J., Cox, B. J., Deacon, B., Heimberg, R. G., Ledley, D. R. et al. (2007). Robust dimensions of anxiety sensitivity: Development and initial validation of the Anxiety Sensitivity Index-3. *Psychological Assessment, 19,* 176–188.

Tillfors, M., Furmark, T., Ekselius, L., & Fredrikson, M. (2001). Social phobia and avoidant personality disorder as related to parental history of social anxiety: A general population study. *Behavior Research and Therapy, 39,* 289–298.

Turk, C. L., Heimberg, R. G., Orsillo, S. M., Holt, C. S., Gitow, A., Street, L. L., et al. (1998). An investigation of gender differences in social phobia. *Journal of Anxiety Disorders, 12,* 209–223.

Turner, S. M., Beidel. D. C., Cooley-Quille, M. R., Woody, S. R., & Messer, S. C. (1994). A multi-component behavioral treatment for social phobia: Social effectiveness therapy. *Behaviour Research and Therapy, 32,* 381–390.

Turner, S. M., Beidel, D. C., Dancu, C. V., & Keys, D. J. (1986). Psychopathology of social phobia and comparison to avoidant personality disorder. *Journal of Abnormal Psychology, 95,* 389–394.

Turner, S. M., Beidel, D. C., & Jacob, R. G. (1994). Social phobia: A comparison of behavior therapy and atenolol. *Journal of Consulting and Clinical Psychology, 62,* 350–358.

Turner, S. M., Johnson, M. R., Beidel, D. C., Heiser, N. A., & Lydiard, R. B. (2003) The Social Thoughts and Beliefs Scale: A new inventory for assessing cognitions in social phobia. *Psychological Assessment, 15,* 384–391.

Weissman, M. M., Bland, R. C., Canino, G. J., Greenwald, S., Lee, C. K., Newman, S. C., et al. (1996). The cross-national epidemiology of social phobia: A preliminary report. *International Clinical Psychopharmacology, 11* (Suppl. 3), 9–14.

Wells, A., Clark, D. M., Salkovskis, P., Ludgate, J., Hackmann, A., & Gelder, M. (1995). Social phobia: The role of in-situation safety behaviors in maintaining anxiety and negative beliefs. *Behavior Therapy, 26,* 153–161.

Westra, H. A., & Dozois, D. J. A. (2006). Preparing clients for cognitive behavioral therapy: A randomized pilot study of motivational interviewing for anxiety. *Cognitive Therapy and Research, 30,* 481–498.

Wittchen, H. U., & Beloch, E. (1996). The impact of social phobia on quality of life. *International Clinical Psychopharmacology, 11* (Suppl. 3), 15–23.

Wittchen, H. U., & Fehm, L. (2003). Epidemiology and natural course of social fears and social phobia. *Acta Psychiatrica Scandinavica Supplementum, 417,* 4–18.

Woody, S. R., & Adessky, R. S. (2002). Therapeutic alliance, group cohesion, and homework compliance during cognitive-behavioral group treatment of social phobia. *Behavior Therapy, 33,* 5–27.

Yonkers, K. A., Bruce, S. E., Dyck, I. R., & Keller, M. B. (2003). Chronicity, relapse, and illness – Course of panic disorder, social phobia, and generalized anxiety disorder: Findings in men and women from 8 years of follow-up. *Depression and Anxiety, 17,* 173–179.

Zimbardo, P. G., Pilkonis, P. A., & Norwood, R. M. (1975). The social disease of shyness. *Psychology Today, 8,* 68–72.

Zimmerman, M., & Mattia, J. I. (2001). A self-report scale to help make psychiatric diagnoses: The Psychiatric Diagnostic Screening Questionnaire (PDSQ). *Archives of General Psychiatry, 58,* 787–794.

Zinbarg, R. E. (1993). Information processing and classical conditioning: Implications for exposure therapy and the integration of cognitive therapy and behavior therapy. *Journal of Behavior Therapy and Experimental Psychiatry, 24,* 129–139.

Appendix: Tools and Resources

The following tools and resources are found in this appendix:
- List of national association in the U.S. and Canada
- List of social anxiety websites and forums
- The Social Phobia Inventory (SPIN)
- Three components of anxiety monitoring form
- Social anxiety thought record form
- List of steps to examine the evidence of cognitive therapy for SAD
- Exposure hierarchy form
- A client handout describing guidelines for effective exposure
- Exposure monitoring form

National Associations in The United States and Canada

Association for Behavioral and Cognitive Therapies
305 Seventh Avenue – 16th Floor
New York, NY 10001-6008
United States
Tel. +1 212-647-1890 or 800-685-2228
Fax +1 212-647-1865
http://www.abct.org

Benefits
- Informative website
- Memberships for professionals only
- Annual conference
- Names of professionals who treat anxiety disorders

Anxiety Disorders Association of America
8730 Georgia Avenue, Suite 600
Silver Spring, MD 20910
United States
Tel: +1 240-485-1035
http://www.adaa.org

Benefits
- Informative website
- Memberships for professionals and consumers
- Annual conference
- Information on anxiety support groups in the United States, Canada, South Africa, Mexico, and Australia
- Names of professionals who treat anxiety disorders in the United States, Canada, and elsewhere

Anxiety Disorders Association of Canada
797 Somerset Street West, Suite 39
Ottawa ON K1R 6R3
Canada
Tel: +1 613-722-0236 or 888-223-2252
Fax: +1 613-722-0374
http:// anxietycanada.ca

Benefits
- Informative website
- Memberships for professionals and consumers
- Occasional national conference
- Links to provincial associations

Social Anxiety Websites and Forums

Shyness Home Page
http://www.shyness.com

Shyness and Social Anxiety Treatment Australia
http://www.socialanxietyassist.com.au/index.shtml

Social Anxiety Support
http://www.socialanxietysupport.com/

Social Phobia/Social Anxiety Association
http://www.socialphobia.org/

Social Phobia World
http://www.socialphobiaworld.com/index.php

Social Phobia Inventory (SPIN)

Description

The SPIN (Davidson, 1998) is a 17-item, self-report questionnaire designed to assess symptoms of SAD. Each item describes a symptom of SAD, and the respondent rates the degree to which he or she has been bothered by the symptom during the previous week on a 5-point scale ranging from 0 (*not at all*) to 4 (*extremely*). Overall, the SPIN has been found to be a reliable and valid tool for assessing the severity of SAD (Antony, Coons, McCabe, Ashbaugh, & Swinson, 2006; Connor et al., 2000). In addition to generating a total score, the SPIN was also designed to generate scores for three subscales: *fear, avoidance,* and *physiological arousal.* Note that factor analytic findings generally do not support these subscales, and usually only total scores are used. Nevertheless, the instructions for computing both the total score and subscale scores are provided below.

Administration and Scoring

The SPIN takes approximately 5 to 10 minutes to administer.
To compute the total score: Sum of all 17 items
To compute the subscale scores:
   Fear – Sum of items 1, 3, 5, 10, 14, 15
   Avoidance – Sum of items 4, 6, 8, 9, 11, 12, 16
   Physiological arousal – Sum of items 2, 7, 13, 17

Interpreting Scores

The mean total score the SPIN in individuals with SAD was found to be 41.1 (standard deviation = 10.2) in one study (Connor et al., 2000), and 44.7 (standard deviation = 14.8) in another study (Antony et al., 2006). The mean score for a nonpsychiatric control group was 12.1 (standard deviation = 9.3; Connor et al., 2000). A cut-off score of 19 has been found to distinguish between individuals with and without SAD with a diagnostic efficiency of 79% (Connor et al., 2000).

References

Antony, M. M., Coons, M. J., McCabe, R. E., Ashbaugh, A. R., & Swinson, R. P. (2006). Psychometric properties of the Social Phobia Inventory: Further evaluation. *Behaviour Research and Therapy, 44,* 1177–1185.

Connor, K. M., Davidson, J. R. T., Churchill, L. E., Sherwood, A., Foa, E., Wesler, R. H. (2000). Psychometric properties of the Social Phobia Inventory (SPIN). *British Journal of Psychiatry, 176,* 379–386.

Social Phobia Inventory (SPIN)®

Please check how much the following problems have bothered you during the past week. Mark only one box for each problem, and be sure to answer all items.

	Not at all 0	A little bit 1	Somewhat 2	Very much 3	Extremely 4
1. I am afraid of people in authority.	☐	☐	☐	☐	☐
2. I am bothered by blushing in front of people.	☐	☐	☐	☐	☐
3. Parties and social events scare me.	☐	☐	☐	☐	☐
4. I avoid talking to people I don't know.	☐	☐	☐	☐	☐
5. Being criticized scares me a lot.	☐	☐	☐	☐	☐
6. Fear of embarrassment causes me to avoid doing things or speaking to people.	☐	☐	☐	☐	☐
7. Sweating in front of people causes me distress.	☐	☐	☐	☐	☐
8. I avoid going to parties.	☐	☐	☐	☐	☐
9. I avoid activities in which I am the center of attention.	☐	☐	☐	☐	☐
10. Talking to strangers scares me.	☐	☐	☐	☐	☐
11. I avoid having to give speeches.	☐	☐	☐	☐	☐
12. I would do anything to avoid being criticized.	☐	☐	☐	☐	☐
13. Heart palpitations bother me when I am around people.	☐	☐	☐	☐	☐
14. I am afraid of doing things when people might be watching.	☐	☐	☐	☐	☐
15. Being embarrassed or looking stupid are among my worst fears.	☐	☐	☐	☐	☐
16. I avoid speaking to anyone in authority.	☐	☐	☐	☐	☐
17. Trembling or shaking in front of others is distressing to me.	☐	☐	☐	☐	☐

Three Components of Anxiety Monitoring Form

Situation	Fear (0–100)	Physical Sensations	Fearful Thoughts and Predictions	Behaviors

Social Anxiety Thought Record

Day and Time	Situation	Anxiety-Provoking Thoughts and Predictions	Anxiety Before (0–100)	Alternative Thoughts and Predictions	Evidence and Realistic Conclusions	Anxiety After (0–100)

Steps for Examining the Evidence in Cognitive Therapy for SAD

1. *Identifying the anxious thought*
   - During my presentation, people will notice my blushing and think that I am strange.

2. *Generating alternative beliefs*
   - Nobody will notice my blushing.
   - Only a small number of people will notice my blushing.
   - People who notice my blushing will think I am feeling hot.
   - People who notice my blushing will think I am feeling unwell.
   - People who notice my blushing will think I am feeling a bit anxious.
   - It is normal to blush sometimes, so people will think nothing of it if they notice me blush.

3. *Examining the evidence*
   Evidence supporting my anxious belief:
   - I believe that my blushing is very extreme.
   - In high school people teased me for blushing on a few occasions.
   - I tend to notice when other people blush.
   Evidence supporting my alternative beliefs:
   - I know a lot of people who blush easily and people don't seem to think they are strange.
   - When I notice other people blushing, I don't think they are strange.
   - Often people do not seem to have noticed me blush when I ask them if it was noticeable.
   - When people have noticed my blushing, they haven't tended to treat me differently.
   - The people in the audience know me well. I can't imagine that their opinions of me would change dramatically based on whether I blush during a single presentation.

4. *Choosing a more realistic belief*
   - Some people may notice my blushing, but it's unlikely that they will think I'm strange.

Adapted from M.M. Antony and R.P. Swinson. (2000). *Phobic Disorders and Panic in Adults: A Guide to Assessment and Treatment*. Washington, DC: American Psychological Association. Used with permission.
This page may be reproduced by the purchaser for clinical use.
From: M.M. Antony & K. Rowa: *Social Anxiety Disorder*, © 2008 Hogrefe & Huber Publishers

Exposure Hierarchy Form

Item Number	Item Description	Fear Rating (0–100)
1		
2		
3		
4		
5		
6		
7		
8		
9		
10		
11		
12		
13		
14		
15		

From: M.M. Antony & K. Rowa: *Social Anxiety Disorder*, © 2008 Hogrefe & Huber Publishers

Client Handout – Guidelines for Effective Exposure

1. *Exposure Practices should be planned, structured, and predictable.* Decide in advance what you will do in the situation and how long you will stay. Plan in advance when you will complete your practice and put it in your schedule. Have a back up plan in case the original plan doesn't work out.

2. *Exposure practices should be repeated frequently and spaced close together.* The more closely spaced the practices, the more fear reduction that you are likely to experience. It is a good idea to practice being in the same situation repeatedly until it becomes easier.

3. *Exposure practices should last long enough to learn that your feared consequences don't occur.* A significant reduction in fear is a good sign that you have stayed long enough (sometimes this can take several hours!).

4. *Exposure pace can be gradual.* In other words, do not assume that you must do the most difficult thing you can imagine right away. On the other hand, be sure to choose practices that are challenging. The more difficult the items that you practice, the quicker you will learn to become more comfortable. Try to choose practices that are challenging but not so difficult that you will not complete them.

5. *Do not use subtle avoidance strategies during exposure practices.* In other words, try to complete the practices without the use of distraction, alcohol, leaving early, avoiding eye contact, and other such strategies.

6. *Rate your fear on a scale from 0 to 100.* When in the feared situation, it can be helpful to pay attention to how you are feeling and to notice the variables that make your anxiety go up and down during the practice.

7. *Try not to fight your fear.* Fighting the fear will have the effect of increasing your anxious feelings. Instead, just let it happen. The worst thing that is likely to happen is that you will feel uncomfortable.

8. *Use the cognitive coping strategies* to counter anxious automatic thoughts during exposure practices.

9. *Expect to feel uncomfortable.* It is perfectly normal to feel awful during initial exposure practices. Also, these practices may leave you feeling tired and anxious afterwards. With repeated practices, these feelings will decrease. Success should *not* be judged by how you felt in the situation. Rather, success should be judged by whether you were able to stay in the situation despite feeling awful.

10. *Use exercises to enhance your anxiety and to draw attention to yourself in the feared situation.* For example, if you fear sweating, wear a heavy sweater. Or, if you fear having others notice your shaky hands, purposely shake your hand while holding a drink. If you are fearful of losing your train of thought, you can purposely allow yourself to have trouble finding the right words during a conversation.

Adapted from M.M. Antony and R.P. Swinson. (2000). *Phobic Disorders and Panic in Adults: A Guide to Assessment and Treatment.* Washington, DC: American Psychological Association. Used with permission.
This page may be reproduced by the purchaser for clinical use.
From: M.M. Antony & K. Rowa: *Social Anxiety Disorder,* © 2008 Hogrefe & Huber Publishers

Exposure Monitoring Form

Describe the Exposure Situation _____   Date and Time _____

Initial Fear Level (0–100) _____   Fear Level at End (0–100) _____   Duration of Exposure _____

Complete before the exposure practice		Complete after the exposure practice
What emotions (e.g., fear, anger, etc.) do I have as I think about doing this exposure?	What anxiety-provoking thoughts, predictions, and assumptions do I have about the exposure? What do I expect will happen during the exposure practice?	What evidence do I have that my fearful thoughts are true?	What was the **outcome** of this practice? What actually happened? What **evidence** did I gain from this practice? How accurate were my original thoughts and predications
			1. Outcome of Practice 2. Evidence Gained

Fear Ratings (0–100)

Provide occasional fear ratings over the course of the exposure practice. For example, for a 20-minute exposure practice, record ratings every 5 minutes or so. For a 2-hour exposure practice, record ratings every 15 minutes or so. Space is provided for a total of 20 ratings over the course of the practice.

1. ____	2. ____	3. ____	4. ____	5. ____	6. ____	7. ____	8. ____	9. ____	10. ____
11. ____	12. ____	13. ____	14. ____	15. ____	16. ____	17. ____	18. ____	19. ____	20. ____

Based on this experience, what exposure practice will you complete next? _____

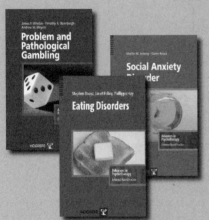